Arthur Donahue

LAST FLIGHT
FROM SINGAPORE

Contents

LAST FLIGHT FROM SINGAPORE

Citation

"This officer carried out many low level reconnaissance sorties and successfully attacked enemy shipping and ground objectives. On one occasion while attacking enemy troops who were attempting a landing in the Singapore area, he silenced the enemy's fire and enabled the rest of the squadron to press home attacks with impunity. He has destroyed several enemy planes."

Chapter I

Parting

I suppose if I had accomplished anything really worth while during the fighting in Singapore and Sumatra, I should now suspect that fate had something to do with my being there, for it was certainly quite by chance that I was sent. However, my accomplishments in the Far East proved to be so small and my attempts at accomplishment so regularly crowned with frustration, that there could hardly have been any design about it.

It all really started with an invitation I received to a party back in England, last autumn (1941)— started with that, and ended with my evacuation from Java in a hospital ship, after being wounded in "the greatest military disaster ever suffered by British arms."

This invitation came from D—, an airdrome about a hundred miles from where I was stationed. The party, it read, was being given as a farewell for the officers of 300 [a fictitious number] Squadron, who were preparing to leave for overseas service.

"300 Squadron?" I thought. "Why, that's Squadron Leader T—'s gang. I must see him if he's going overseas; I'll have to take that in."

Squadron Leader T— had once been my flight commander and was an especial friend of mine. He must have had me invited.

So it was that I knocked off work at noon of the day of the party, having arranged to take twenty-four hours off and to borrow a little training plane for the trip to D—.

I was pilot in a Spitfire squadron at that time, doing reconnaissance work over the Channel and northern France, a job in which I was completely happy. I was at a pleasant station with a swell bunch of fellows, and the work was most absorbing and exciting, with frequent opportunities for us to accomplish something and break into the communiques.

I was in extra high spirits that noon and couldn't help whistling gaily as I stripped off my mae west (life jacket), hung it on my nail in the pilot's hut, and put on my collar and tie (which are never worn when we're flying, because they interfere with looking around). Calling a gay "See you tomorrow!" to the fellows, I hurried outside, mounted my bicycle, and pedaled away. A fifteen minute ride, following the macadam taxi strip around the edge of the airdrome to the gate and then up a winding tree-lined country road for a couple of miles, brought me to the house where we were billeted, and I hurried upstairs to change clothes.

The exhilarating feeling of looking forward to a full twenty-four hours of relaxation, free from dangers and responsibilities, was enhanced for me just now by pride in the memory of having done a little good work during the morning. Alan and I had been nosing along the French coast about midmorning, the cannons and machine-guns of our Spitfires loaded for anything we might encounter.

This time it had been a German motor launch of some sort, and the picture as we went in to attack was still fresh in my mind— the boat dead in my sights a few hundred yards ahead as I came in, skimming low over the sea. Then the terrific barking of my cannons and the roar of my machine-guns as I pressed the firing button, the glimpses from the corners of my eyes of wicked white flame lancing the hot grey smoke clouds whipping back from my cannon muzzles, the exciting stench of gunpowder smoke; then the sight of my first shots striking, falling a little short and throwing up great showers of spray that nearly hid the boat; then the rest of my bullets striking home— brilliant white flashes of cannon shells, and the red sparklet effect of scores of explosive machine-gun bullets, dancing up and down over the bow and the low bridge, and over the queer little square superstructure with a big swastika painted on each side.

Then I was breaking away in a violent turn to avoid colliding after I'd closed to point-blank, and turning in my cockpit to watch Alan following in with his attack, his distant Spitfire looking wicked and panther-like from in front, as only a Spitfire can; seeing the row of little lights break out, flashing along the front of his wings, and the twin streams of grey cannon-smoke puffs ripping back from his machine like taut strings of soft grey beads; then the answering clouds of spray thrown up about the boat by his bullets and the blinking of white cannon-shell flashes all over its hull. We didn't dare wait to see what became of the boat, but we wouldn't have given much for its chances of remaining afloat very long!

After that the two of us— scooting for home side by side and low down over the waves as hard as we could go, engines bellowing raucously at full throttle, and controls stiff with the speed; squirming in our cockpits to look furtively backwards for signs of 109's (Messerschmitts) in pursuit, feeling for all the world like a couple of kids who'd just stolen a watermelon! For we were only two, and we'd got away with this in clear weather without cloud protection along the part of France where the Luftwaffe had its greatest concentration of fighters, hundreds of them. Besides, we had done this right under the noses of the coastal anti-aircraft guns, and so quickly they didn't have time to fire a single shot at us!

As no signs of pursuit appeared we breathed deeper and deeper, until finally the French coast had faded away behind, and then the lighthouse tower of Dungeness slowly emerged from the haze ahead of us, looking beautiful and friendly because it meant that we had got away with "another one."

Upstairs in my room now, I shed my rough blue "battle dress," and after bathing and cleaning up donned my "Sunday best" uniform which my batman had laid out, freshly pressed, with buttons polished and gleaming. Taking the overnight bag which I'd already packed, I left the house and pedaled back to the Mess, hoping I wasn't too late for lunch.

I almost didn't make the trip to the party after all-in which case I wouldn't be writing this story— for a strong northwest wind was blowing, and over the lunch table, Moses, just down from a patrol, told me he thought I'd have trouble making it to D—. He'd noticed thunderstorms and low cloud in that direction. So after lunch I rang up John, our duty pilot, asking him for the weather to D—, and he confirmed what Moses had told me. Thunderstorms, with fog right down to the ground in places, blocked the route, and there wasn't a hope of getting through for the time being.

As a result I just about decided to call off the trip and ring up Squadron Leader T— to tell him good-bye on the phone; but then I thought I'd wait and see if the weather might improve. It did toward mid-afternoon, and John rang me up to tell me that Operations said I could try it if I liked, so off I went.

Even then I nearly didn't make it, for, after I'd flown about fifty or sixty miles, the weather got thick and dark all around. A thunderstorm loomed ahead with white curtains of rain hanging to the ground. I was miserably cold already in the open cockpit of the little Moth biplane, and sick of shivering, my face blue and my nose running, and of bouncing around in the rough air which tossed the little trainer about like a chip; sick above all of the slow speed — exasperating, since I was used to streaking about the countryside at two and three hundred miles an hour in Spitfires.

So I almost said "Nuts to it!" again and turned back; but then I saw a lighter patch ahead on my left and decided to make a try at it. By swinging off my course and edging close to the London balloon barrage I managed finally to get by the bad area, and then it was clear sailing the rest of the way to D—, where I landed triumphantly.

There I found more bad luck in store for me, for Squadron Leader T— was gone; not only that, but there was no party either!

The duty pilot gave me the news, as soon as I reported to him in the watch office and told him what I'd come for. "Well, I'm awfully sorry about this," he said. "Didn't you get our wire? We telegraphed everyone who'd been invited and told them the party 'd been postponed. You see, the boys who are going overseas have all had their embarkation leave extended and they aren't back yet. Yes, Squadron Leader T—'s away, too. I don't know just when he expects to be back."

Well, that was something. I'd completely wasted a trip up here just because of a telegram that somehow did not reach me. It had been a darned cold trip, too.

I rang up the local Operations Room, and got permission to return to my home airdrome as soon as my machine was ready.

The "Station Duty Flight" (a crew of mechanics whose job was to care for visiting planes) were refuelling my airplane and checking over one of the magnetos which had bothered a little on the way, and while waiting for them to finish their work I stood around toasting myself in front of the wall-type electric heaters in the little watch office, for I was chilled through and through.

Presently one of the mechanics came in to tell me the news. "I'm sorry, sir, but I don't think we can get that magneto fixed for you today. There seems to be something wrong inside it, and we'll have to take it apart."

"All right," I answered, "it doesn't make much difference. I'll stay here overnight then." And so I did.

All these chance occurrences that led up to my staying at D— that night, also led to my living the rest of the events of this story; for next morning before I left, Squadron Leader T— returned from his leave, and in the ensuing visit talked me into joining the rest of his squadron to go overseas.

Not directly; but he told me that he'd like to have me with his squadron, and I said that, for my part, I was game, if he could get me transferred. So he rang up the officer in charge of postings at Group Headquarters, who said that the time was very short, but if I were willing to forego embarkation leave he'd do what he could about it and let us know. So we let it stand that way. I flew back to my home airdrome, and after telling my C.O. and the other pilots of my squadron that I might be leaving them soon, I went to work.

Squadron Leader T— hadn't entirely talked me into volunteering for overseas service; I'd thought of it occasionally before. It was mainly that the opportunity was presented to me at a time when it sounded particularly attractive. Winter was fast approaching with its weeks of foggy weather and inactivity in England, while big things appeared to be in the offing abroad. Japan wasn't in the war yet, of course, but Hitler's armies in Russia had reached the northeastern shores of the Black Sea and a drive down through the Caucasus Mountains looked imminent; besides, we'd heard rumors and opinions (which soon proved correct) that one side or the other would be starting something big in Libya before long. It seemed likely that the squadron would be sent to one or the other of these areas and that we'd have a chance to write some history wherever we went.

A couple of days after my meeting with Squadron Leader T—, the officer in charge of postings telephoned me that my transfer had been arranged and that I was to report at D— in two days' time. It was what I wanted, but I realized with a shock that it was going to be very hard to say goodbye to this place and to the pals I had worked and flown and fought with all these months. They seemed to feel the same way about it, too. Some of us drove to Dover that night, to take in a vaudeville show at that famous old theater, the "Dover Hippodrome." It was my last night out with the gang.

The Huns staged a dive-bombing raid on Dover while we were on the way. We could see the anti-aircraft bursts in the sky and the great yellow flashes of the bombs below, so we parked for a few minutes on a hill overlooking the town, watching the display and listening to the drone of engines, the explosions of bombs, and the barking of anti-aircraft guns, until it all quieted down again, and we drove on.

During the show I got all the fellows to autograph my programme, and kept it for a remembrance of my last night out with them. The performance consisted of dancing and other numbers by the "Saucy Lovelies," humorous acts and monologues by Hal Monty, music by "Butch and Buddy" — a couple of air-raid orphans picked up in a Liverpool shelter by the manager of the show. There were also juggling, "Poses by Eve" (enough said), and other numbers.

I had one or two patrols next morning, which I don't remember much about, except that I flew with a strange heavy lump in my breast. When noon came, my flight was off for the rest of the day. But I took one more hop anyway, as a sort of farewell jaunt with my old Spitfire. I'd had the same machine for nearly six months— ever since it was brand new— and I felt very attached to it. I'd had the words *Message from Minnesota* painted on its side, because that is my home state.

I took off, and flew up and down the middle of the Straits of Dover for a while, flying above and below and through a blanket of thick, fluffy clouds that covered most of the Straits, hoping someone might come out from the other side for a fight. Then I spent a little time searching around the French coast for a couple of "bandits," which Control told me (via radio) were patrolling in the Cap Gris Nez area; but I didn't see anything of them and finally Control informed me they'd gone back inland, so I gave up and headed homeward, taking one last look across at France as I circled my drome before landing. Someone else would fly my airplane from now on, and he'd remove the name I had on it. But I consoled myself with the hope that soon I'd be flying a new *Message from Minnesota II* somewhere, anyway.

That afternoon I packed. Next morning, one of Squadron Leader T—'s pilots came down to fetch me in a training plane and I flew to D— with him, planning to return later and get my heavy luggage by train. At D— I found that all the pilots of my new squadron were back from their embarkation leave, and I had a chance to get acquainted with them. There were three other Americans in the crowd, two Californians and one from Florida, all swell fellows. The California boys were Don G— and Red C—; the latter was to become the squadron's first ace. Kleck, who came from Florida, had quit a good government job in Washington to join as a recruit the Royal Canadian Air Force. There were five New Zealanders also, besides boys from Australia, Rhodesia, Canada, and, as we put it, "even a few Englishmen," who were generally known as "the foreigners."

All were getting "shots in the arm" from a doctor that day, and I joined them in "sick quarters" to get the first of a series of shots for yellow fever, tetanus, typhoid, and other tropical diseases, with the result that I nursed a sore arm for a day or so.

The next couple of days I spent doing some practice flying to get acquainted with the Hurricane fighters this squadron used, as I had never flown Hurricanes before; and after that I got a couple of days off to wind up my affairs.

The first of these two days I spent in London, taking care of some financial matters and shopping for various things, including a "tropical trunk" — all steel for protection against insects.

Before I left London the next morning I stopped in at the American Eagle Club for a cup of coffee, and there met Tex M—, a friend of mine from Waxahachie, Texas, who had been flying in the American Eagle Squadron. He told me he had just been posted to Singapore and was on embarkation leave, prior to sailing. I told him I was going overseas, too, but didn't know where, and we wished each other luck.

I took a train for my old squadron's base, arriving in late afternoon. It was cloudy and blustery and chilly, with a few snowflakes in the air, and when I got out to the drome, in a taxi, there seemed to be little going on. I visited my flight's dispersal hut first, to get a few belongings I'd left there, and found that the flight were off duty and only a couple of boys around.

All the Spitfires were standing in their dispersal bays, like tired cavalry horses asleep, each as familiar to me as an old comrade, bringing me memories.

There was Paddy's old machine, 'N,' which had always been lucky. Paddy had shot down at least two 109's with it. Chris was using it the day he was out on a reco (reconnaissance flight), and surprised a formation of three 109's over Le Touquet, dropping on them out of the sun and shooting down two before they knew what had happened, and then coming home so excited he couldn't talk, having completely forgotten to finish his reco! Gilli was flying it the day he blundered into a whole bunch of 109's in a thick haze low over the sea north of Nieuport, shot down one, damaged a second, and got away unscathed, leaving the rest dog-fighting with each other in their confusion.

There was Chris's old machine 'P,' Gilli's 'U,' Roy's 'V,' Alan's 'T,' and all the rest, including 'S'— the one everybody hated because it didn't perform as well as the others. And of course there was my own 'O,' my *Message from Minnesota*, which I knew and loved the best. Personalities, all of them, to me; for one of us will fly another's airplane when his own is laid up for repairs, checks, and so on, and I knew all the peculiarities of each.

There wasn't one in whose cockpit I hadn't experienced unforgettable thrills and scares, flown through unbelievable scenes of grandeur and beauty among and above the clouds. And how often I'd seen each of them taxiing back to its place after a flight across the Channel, displaying evidence of a battle fought or a target attacked— the tattered remnants of what had been fabric covers for the holes until they were shot away, fluttering about the holes for the machine guns in the wings, and the ugly bared cannon muzzles, dirtied with powder smoke, their covers likewise shot away. Sometimes it was I who taxied in with my machine bearing these signs, my heart still pounding, while I grinned behind my oxygen mask with an amount of pride proportional to whatever it was that I had accomplished.

And now it was all over. I was saying good-bye to it all and to them all, and it was very hard. Sergeant Y—, also an American, was flying my machine now. He came around while I was there and said he was going to taxi it across to the hangar for a thirty-hour inspection, and I asked him if he'd mind my taxiing it over for him. He said O.K. So after I was through collecting my things I climbed into the cockpit of my old friend, started up, and taxied across the field. When I stopped in front of the hangar and shut off the engine, I thought I should make a ceremony of leaving it for the last time, then realized how foolish I was, and jumped out and walked away without looking back.

The wind was still blowing and the sky overcast that night as I rode along the dark highway and through the blacked-out city with the friend who drove me to the station, and my heart was heavier than ever. I'd planned to stay overnight and take a morning train, but a telephone call at suppertime informed me that our date of embarkation had been advanced and that I had to take the train right away.

It meant I hardly had time to say good-bye to any of my pals, which was probably just as well because I know I'd have broken down. I wanted at least to see Chris, and I'd made a hasty trip to the country house where he and his wife were staying, but had found it dark, silent, and empty save for their little dog, "Rocky," who alone answered when I knocked, and who barked his good-bye as I

14

walked back across the lawn. They had gone away somewhere for the afternoon and evening, not knowing that I was coming.

When I got on the train, I could hardly keep my eyes dry as I fumbled my way into one of the darkened compartments and slumped down, utterly miserable, beside a couple of soldiers going on leave, who moved their rifles to make room for me on the seat.

Hoping to see something familiar, I pulled the curtains aside for a last look after we got out of town, and, as if the elements sympathized with me, I found that the clouds had blown away and that the countryside now was bathed in brilliant moonlight. The airdrome was out of sight from the railway, but "Old Baldy," a high, rounded hill that was a landmark beside it, was plainly visible and I took a long last look at it, trying to photograph it in my memory. Then I replaced the curtain, resolving to keep my mind on the future.

Chapter II

Impatience

I suppose that if you rounded up a score of two-year-old colts from a Montana range and penned them in a half-acre corral for a few weeks during the fresh new days of spring, you could get an idea from watching them of how we fighter pilots felt and acted during our long imprisonment aboard ship.

Accustomed as we were to flying an hour or two in going from one place to another, this business of spending days and even weeks between stops was appalling. We read until our eyes ached, played cards, argued endlessly about everything from air tactics to women's suffrage. Our tempers grew shorter until we were constantly flying off the handle at one another over insignificant little things, so that our C.O. was at his wit's end trying to keep the peace— and still our voyage had scarcely started!

The lazy, ambling motion of our ship, with its top speed of fully fifteen miles an hour, was exasperating. Didn't it know we had a war to fight? I spent so much time leaning on the rail, watching the endless acres of waves crawling past, and wondering how there could be so many of them all in one ocean, that I thought I'd be developing a permanent stoop.

I suppose it was only natural that we started seeing Gremlins. These are the little men, about four or five inches tall, who live in the sky and have been a legend in the R.A.F. ever since the first pilot took off with a hangover in the last war, saw one perched on his windshield making faces at him, and swore off Paris night clubs and French champagne for the duration.

I heard about them shortly after joining the R.A.F., and asked a pilot of the last war, who was adjutant at my station, if he could tell me what they looked like.

"Well," he said, "it really depends on what sort of shape you're in when you see them, old boy. Of course you modern pilots don't drink, so you're always in the same shape. Why, as I remember, they're rather sly appearing little chaps, with long white beards, dressed in green waistcoats and tall green hats. Most of them don't intend to be mean, just playful — except the one I used to see in peacetime, perched on my pillow on mornings after a night out in town—"

He shook his head reminiscently. "That was a wicked one, absolutely ferocious to look at, too. He had a little sharp dagger that he'd waken me with by poking me just above the eyes. I'd start to raise up, and 'Bam!' he'd hit me on the back of the head with a hammer twice as long as he was. Then the little blightuh would run down to the foot of my bed and sit there laughing at me. I'd growl at him and tell him to hop it, but he'd just sit there and make a face at me. I'd close my eyes and try to sleep again, and a minute later he'd be back, to give me another working over!" He shook his head again. "That one was a regular outlaw, but most of them aren't too bad if you treat them right."

I think I should add here that these little fellows are credited with many unusual gifts, including great strength and the ability to fly — supposed to be due to their special diet of spandule, or aerial seaweed (airweed).

If you ask a student pilot about Gremlins, he'll probably tell you of the ones who hide in training planes during flight. When the student is coming in to land, they all run out to the end of one wing and, just when he's about to touch down for a perfect landing, give a great heave upwards, tipping his machine over so that the opposite wing hits the ground. Or the ones who cause crackups by moving trees or telephone poles in front of you when you're gliding in to land, or push other airplanes into your way when you're taxiing on the ground. Or the tribe known as the "Ground Wallopers," who are responsible when a student bounces on landing; they shove your control stick forward or backward just as you're touching down, causing you either to hit the ground too hard or else to zoom up too high and pancake.

Another gang of them have an ingenious and destructive prank which they sometimes work even on experienced pilots. Two of them stand by in your cockpit, out of sight, while you're flying, and when you move the lever to lower your wheels in preparation for landing, one of them sneaks up and throws the lever back into neutral so that your wheels stay up, retracted. Then the other one, hiding behind your instrument panel, rewires the position indicator for your wheels, so that it shows wheels down when in reality they're still up, and you glide in for a perfect crackup, landing your plane on its belly.

After the dust clears away, while the crash truck is approaching and you're still sitting in your cockpit, gazing stupidly at your bent or broken propeller and wings, the two little fellows jump up on your windshield, stick their tongues out at you in a final gesture of insolence, and vanish, leaving you to figure out how you're going to explain it all to the C.O. At least, that's how some pilots claim it happens.

There's no end to the kinds of tricks they'll pull if they have it in for you. They hide behind your compass and hold magnets by it, causing the compass to point the wrong way, and you get lost. They steal your maps, hide in your radio set, and bang on it with hammers so you can't hear any messages. They sneak into your gas tank and drink up your gasoline, steal the bullets from your machine guns and put in corks, paint Messerschmitts on top of your cockpit hood to scare the life out of you, and so on, until they've driven you half crazy.

The first one was discovered on the ship by our C.O. one evening when we were all gathered in the Officers' Wardroom (lounge), with most of the ship's officers. One of the officers, who was called Dinty, was just going to sit down in a comfortable chair when our C.O. grabbed him and called out in alarm, "Look out — Don't sit down, Dinty! You'll squash him— Look!" He was pointing at the middle of the seat, and we all looked. Sure enough, there was the cutest little Gremlin, about middle age, curled up fast asleep, his head pillowed on a tobacco pouch which the navigator had left there.

Dinty, who of course couldn't see it because he wasn't a pilot, was absolutely bewildered. He gazed first at us, then at the chair, then back at us— all grouped around and staring.

Someone said, "S-sh— We mustn't wake him up!" and that was too much. With a frightened expression on his face, Dinty retreated to the bar for a quick one.

The Gremlin awoke presently, to follow us when we went down for supper, where he amused us while we were waiting to be served, by cavorting about the room, climbing up on the table and running up and down its length, until he finally tripped over a spoon and fell headfirst into a glass of water. Ambrose rescued him then, lifting him out tenderly by the coat collar with his thumb and forefinger, and setting him out to dry on an empty plate— all to the complete consternation of the naval officers present!

After that, we were frequently visited by one or more of them. One night, two of them were playing about the Wardroom, with all of us watching, and they climbed into the recess in the wall in front of a porthole. Kleck got an inspiration and called, "Look out! They're trying to open the porthole!" Whereupon we all rushed to stop them, for the portholes must be kept tightly closed at night to prevent any traces of light showing. Sure enough, the two little chaps had hold of the big brass wing-nut, one at each end, and were just going to start unscrewing it!

Our C.O. reprimanded them severely, while they listened, with heads hanging and guilty looks on their faces, no doubt wondering if it wouldn't be best to lock us in our cabins. Then we showed them the proper way out for Gremlins— through the ventilator pipe.

We never learned what our original destination was to have been, for one of the great events of history, which was to change it, occurred while we were docked at a port of call.

We heard the news on a Sunday evening when most of us had been away from the ship, attending a movie put on in a shed by the docks for the ship's company of a large warship that was docked near us. Returning to our own ship after the show we were met on the ladder by Red (one of the two Americans from California), his face flushed with excitement, shouting the electrifying words, "America's at war! The Japs have raided Hawaii! Here, read this!" He was waving a wireless message in our faces. It was a general message to all British ships, and read:

"COMMENCE HOSTILITIES WITH JAPAN REPEAT JAPAN AT ONCE"

Chapter III

Our "Road to Singapore"

I felt dazed and overwhelmed. After all the fighting that we Americans in the R.A.F. had been through, believing that we were helping to make this unnecessary, it had come at last, all in a twinkling, and our country was committed to take part in the slaughter.

In the Wardroom we drank a toast with the British officers, to our new alliance. Then later, at midnight, we gathered around the radio to listen to detail after terrible detail of the world-shaking events that had happened in the last few hours.

Everyone was subdued — we Americans because of the tragedy it spelled for our country, and the others because we felt it would lengthen the war to have Japan added to our enemies. The only bright side for us Americans was knowing that we wouldn't be outlaws any more in the eyes of our own country — as we were when I went home on leave to the States the previous winter and wasn't allowed to wear my uniform.

We remained in port for several more days, and it was during this time that Don, the other Californian besides Red, got separated from us. He had a chance to do some flying one day, and in the course of his trip his plane force-landed in a neutral country and he was interned. We never saw him again.

He was to escape finally; and months later, on America's Memorial Day, I was to lay a wreath against a wooden cross with his name on it, erected beside a hole in a little paddy field in a Ceylonese jungle where he had crashed on Easter Sunday, shot down by Japanese fighters in the defense of Ceylon.

Finally we put to sea again, and there followed many more monotonous days. We pilots had to do "gun watches" on the ship, providing the crews for two of the ship's pompom anti-aircraft guns, working in four-hour shifts.

Personally, I have always felt that anti-aircraft guns should be abolished, and Kleck grumbled that this was like asking Charlie McCarthy to take care of a pair of woodpeckers; but we endeavored to subordinate our sentiments and do the job properly.

Actually, we found it rather interesting to learn how to operate these things, after the considerable experience which some of us had had in dodging their fire. The Germans use this type of gun as well as the British, and Vic, for example, still bore scars on his face from one which he failed to dodge.

We sailed into warm tropical seas, where we changed from our blue uniforms into light "tropical dress" of open-necked khaki shirts, khaki shorts, and tan-colored topees instead of caps; and we slept in hammocks on deck because it was too hot in our cabins.

At night the sea was "phosphorescent," one of the wonders of nature which most of us had never seen. Every disturbance in the water caused little flaky green lights to flash beneath the surface, so that the water churned from the ship's sides seemed full of fireflies. Every whitecap was a shower of fiery little green jewels; every fish left a trail like a small green skyrocket in the darkness, and the wake of the ship was like a great convulsive mass of colored fire.

It was on one of these nights, while on watch, that I got my first torpedo scare. I had been leaning over the rail by my gun for a long time, idly watching the lovely show, when suddenly I thought I heard a hissing noise. Looking up, I was terrified to see a huge trail of phosphorescence coming in a straight line toward the ship, scarcely a hundred yards away. I just seemed to freeze, inside and out, as if hypnotized by the sight, as it streaked on, cutting just beneath the waves and straight for the middle of the ship. It came straight as a die until less than twenty yards away, when it suddenly executed a sharp turn, in the most unorthodox manner for torpedoes! Then it started following along beside the ship so that I could see its outline, illuminated by the phosphorescence, and I recognized it as a big porpoise!

When my breath came back, I called the other boys to look. Soon we saw not one porpoise but several; then more and more joined up until there were all of fifty swimming beside us, mostly in pairs, gamboling about and converting the dark water for two or three hundred yards out into a fairyland of curving, swirling green skyrockets. They followed along with us for fifteen or twenty minutes, one of the weirdest and most beautiful shows I've ever seen. Then, little by little, they dispersed and disappeared into the darkness.

Another morning Kleck mistook a piece of floating wood in the distance and shouted "Periscope!" at the top of his lungs, with the result that "Action Stations" was sounded on the ship's alarm system and everyone was in an uproar, including the captain, who'd been taking a bath in his cabin and came bounding up onto the bridge with less dignity than speed, clad only in a bath towel.

We were still in complete ignorance of our eventual destination, when finally we were transferred onto a fair-sized warship, along with the pilots of another squadron, which I will call 175 [a fictitious number] Squadron; they are to play a part in the rest of this story.

We now were able to guess that we were being taken somewhere in the Far East, although no one knew. Then, after we had been at sea for a couple of days, we pilots and all the ship's company not on duty were assembled on deck one evening for a lecture.

It began with a talk by the First Lieutenant, on the Far Eastern situation. Using a large map for reference, he showed us where the Japanese had attacked in the Philippines as well as in Borneo and other islands, and reviewed the situation there. Next, he pointed to where they had invaded Burma and were working toward Rangoon, and last of all to Northern Malaya, where they were pushing down the long Malay Peninsula toward Singapore, at its southern tip. Everything hung on Singapore. If it fell, the enemy would be able to conquer the Dutch East

Indies, which would give them rubber, tin, and oil that they needed to continue the war.

Then the Captain spoke, outlining for the benefit of his crew the work which the ship was to perform in this many-sided campaign. We thought it was a considerate gesture on his part to take his crew into confidence this way— the sort of thing that probably accounted for the wonderful spirit we had already noticed among the entire personnel of his ship.

But we pilots were impatient to learn what was to become of us. It was obvious that the ship was taking us to some place out there, but there were a dozen theaters of operation where fighter squadrons would be needed. Naturally, our highest hopes were that we might get to Singapore itself.

The Captain gave us the answer to that, too, at the close of his talk. "Our Royal Air Force guests are going to leave us at" he named a place in the Dutch East Indies, "where they will get their airplanes. I understand they are then to fly the rest of the way to Singapore, which is their destination!"

A cheer went up from our crowd. We all wanted action, and now we had drawn the jackpot!

About all I remember of the trip across the Indian Ocean is that the sea was always smooth and the days were always hot, sultry, and endless. We didn't even have ambition enough to see Gremlins any more. Our one diversion was swimming, in a canvas pool rigged up on the quarter-deck, which served to cool us off a little. But we were thankful, anyway, that we were on a fast ship, making twice the speed that a trooper would have.

On the evening before we pilots were to be disembarked, the Captain gave a brief talk over the ship's loud-speaker system, stressing the idea that the eyes of the world were focused on the battle we were joining, and bidding us "good-bye, good luck, and good hunting!" We were quite impressed, and I hoped fervently that our squadron would make a good name for itself in the events to come.

Each of our squadrons was up to full strength of twenty-four pilots (giving a reserve of 100 per cent over the normal flying strength of twelve), so there were forty-eight pilots altogether; and the forty-eight were now divided into three groups of sixteen for the trip to Singapore.

I am not permitted to say where we disembarked and got our airplanes. Suffice it to say, that on a sunny morning a few days later the sixteen pilots of my group landed on the municipal airport of Batavia, the principal city in Java, all of us flying brand-new Hurricane II fighters.

This airport was a stopping point in peacetime for K.L.M., the big Dutch airline, and they had a modern passenger terminal, complete with restaurant, waiting room, and bar where I got the first Coca-Cola I'd tasted since leaving America.

We had lunch, and then took off on the next leg of our trip, a flight of three hundred miles or so northwest to a jungle airdrome in Sumatra.

It was a beautiful trip, for the sun was out and the fertile, well-cultivated farmlands of Java appeared rich and green as we cruised over them. There were scattered fluffy clouds under us at low altitude that glistened softly in the sunlight and set off the beauty of the landscape underneath. Then the seacoast, the sea a beautiful blue-green and the white-capped waves gleaming in long lines of snowy crest as they collapsed majestically along the beaches far below us, in all the splendor of color that you see in technicolor pictures of South Sea Islands.

On out across the sea for half an hour or so and then Sumatra, a far different kind of country from Java. This was where everyone said, "If you ever have a forced landing, you've just HAD it!" No cultivated farm lands here. No sign of any kind of civilization. Just endless dark flat jungle stretching off into the steamy horizon in all directions, broken only at great intervals by some silvery stream winding its way across our course and off into the distance. Many, many miles of this, until at last a broken patch appeared ahead of us, and as we neared this it took shape as an airdrome cleared out of the jungle— our stopping point.

As we circled the field before landing, I noticed a strange type of four-engined bomber parked on the ground. It looked like pictures I'd seen of the American Flying Fortress bombers, and I wondered if it could really be an American plane out here in the war zone. I knew America was in the war now, but somehow I just couldn't connect the Stars and Stripes and American uniforms with the awfulness of real fighting.

But when I landed and taxied past the bomber, I saw that it really was so. There was the American insignia of white star over red and blue circles on the sides of the fuselage, seeming very strange to me now after having seen only British and German insignia for so long. There were the strange, light tan uniforms and caps of U.S. Army officers and men around the machine, and they gave me a queer thrill. The men were starting their engines then, and before I had time to park my machine and climb out, they were already taxiing down the field to take off, so I didn't get to talk to them. I was told they didn't belong here and had only landed for gas.

It was too late for us to go any farther that day, so after getting our airplanes serviced and put away, we prepared to stay for the night. This airdrome was simply a couple of enormous runways cleared in the jungle, which grew thickly right up to the edge of the field on all sides. Little "bays" for parking airplanes were cut back into the trees, so that when a machine was parked and a few branches thrown over the top it was effectively concealed from the air.

The R.A.F. were just getting established here, and the Officers' Mess was a large wooden shed with concrete floor, and wooden benches and tables for us to eat at. We lined up at mealtime and drew tea in tin cups from a big boiler, and dipped stew from another boiler into tin plates. Bread, margarine, canned strawberry jam, fresh bananas and pineapples completed our fare.

We slept in camp cots and learned the intricacies of enclosing ourselves in those overhung mosquito-netting affairs which all beds have in tropical places; you've probably seen them in the movies. It's not as difficult as it looks, I found; the sides simply tuck in under the edges of the mattress all around, so that to get in you just pull out one side of the netting, then tuck it back under after you're inside.

The air had been very hot and muggy when we landed, but during the night there were little rains accompanied by some thunder and lightning every hour or so, and it became comfortably cool. However, by the time we got up next morning it was hot and steamy just as before.

That day the weather was too questionable for us to continue to Singapore, so we laid over, and most of us spent the day working on our airplanes. Our machines were brand new, having just been shipped out from England, and there were numerous things to take care of before they would be in fighting condition.

Among other things, all the machine guns were heavily coated inside and out with a special grease to resist corrosion on the long sea journey. I spent most of the day working with some armorers on my airplane, removing and disassembling its twelve guns, carefully cleaning all the parts in gasoline, greasing and oiling the parts properly for service, and then reassembling, installing, and loading them.

We worked beside the airplane, sitting on empty gasoline cans, retreating under the wings to work during the frequent showers that swept across. And while we worked, by chatting with these armorers who had all been in the fighting zone in Malaya until recently, I gradually assimilated some of the picture of what lay ahead for us.

It was from them that I first heard of the new Navy Zero fighter ("Navy-naughts" as we called them at that time), which is to the Jap air force what the Messerschmitt 109 is to the Luftwaffe. These fighters, while not as fast as our Hurricanes, were a sleek little job nonetheless, with great maneuverability and an exceptional cruising range. They carried extra fuel tanks under the wings, that could be jettisoned for combat, and they could operate more than three hundred miles from their bases. They were usually armed with light and heavy machine guns, although some had twenty-millimeter cannons. While our fighters were a match for them individually, we had to expect to be badly outnumbered ordinarily when we engaged them.

One of the armorers, a sergeant, had been an air gunner on Lockheed bombers until recently, and it was from him that I got most of the information about the Navy Zeros. He had destroyed one of them in combat, himself.

They told me the Jap bombers seemed to be good machines, too, and could fly at more than twenty thousand feet with full bomb loads. Much of their bombing was directed against airdromes, the raids usually being carried out by three squadrons of nine planes each in one wing — twenty-seven in all. They flew in beautiful close formation, and when attacking airdromes they did "pattern bombing," all letting their bombs go at once so that they plastered the whole area evenly.

They said the raids were terrifying affairs, but caused surprisingly few casualties. The soil in Malaya and Singapore is so damp and soggy that there is little blast effect from even the heaviest bombs. Ordinary small "slit trenches," three or four feet deep and a couple of feet wide, were all that were used normally for shelters; and often heavy bombs had landed within a couple of yards of a trench and the men suffered nothing worse than a shower of damp earth. In addition to their heavy bombs, the enemy dropped lots of devilish little "anti-personnel" bombs, about fifty pounders, which exploded just as they touched the ground, and threw shrapnel in all directions.

The latest news was that the enemy were less than fifty miles from Singapore Island, and the only airdromes we had left were the four that were situated on the island. It looked as if we had a tough fight ahead of us, which, after all, was just what we wanted.

By the following afternoon the weather had improved enough so that we could go on, and we took off on the last leg of our trip, another three hundred and fifty miles to Singapore itself.

There were two Blenheim bombers making the trip with us, and by previous arrangement we simply followed in formation with them, letting them find the way because they were better equipped for navigating. After taking off, we grouped around them in sections of four, circled the airdrome once to get organized in formation, and headed out across the jungle again— this time nearly straight north.

After the first fifty miles we began to see the coastline in the distance on our right, at first paralleling our course and then gradually angling closer; and it was a little relief to know it was there anyway, to head for in case of engine trouble. We all dreaded the thought of having to land in this jungle.

After perhaps an hour we crossed the coastline and droned out on our one-hundred-and-fifty-mile stretch of overwater flying, across the Straits of Malacca. This wasn't really open sea, as I could see on my map, for it was broken by small islands scattered along most of the way, so that we were seldom out of sight of at least one or two of them.

By this time I was getting tired and stiff from being cramped in one position and I squirmed in my seat, loosened my straps, and tried to do some primitive setting-up exercises for relief. I'd gone for so long without flying that the posture was hard to get used to again. My engine, throttled down almost to idling speed to keep pace with the slower bombers, purred endlessly on the same note, which was broken only when I held my head to one side of the cockpit and got the staccato crackling of the exhausts from that bank of cylinders. Like most of the rest I flew with my sliding cockpit hood open to keep cool, for the sun was out and the air hot; we were actually crossing the equator on this very hop, Singapore being only eighty miles north of it.

This was late in January, and I thought how different it must be back home in Minnesota, where it was midwinter, the thermometer by the door of our house probably showing zero or below, the ground frozen hard, and the countryside covered deep in snow. Right now my folks might be outdoors, bundled in heavy clothes and overshoes, beating their hands together and rubbing their cheeks and noses to keep them from going numb. And yet here I was at the same time, my clothes and the inside of my helmet damp and sticky with sweat, yearning more than anything else for an ice-cold Coke or Orange Crush!

I was leading a section of four, the three others formating on me loosely, their tiredness evidencing itself in the way each of them slowly drifted about in the formation, sometimes lagging behind, then getting too much speed and drifting up too far ahead. Once Artie S— came up beside me for a moment, and I could see his face, with a dopey expression on it as if he were half asleep. We had our oxygen masks unfastened from our faces to keep cooler, so I could see when he grinned across at me, and I grinned back.

After a long time the sky grew darker ahead. The Blenheims started losing altitude, and we did too— keeping formation with them. Then the unmistakable dim outline of land began to emerge along the darkened horizon, and we knew that after months of travel our destination was at last in sight. We began passing under heavy, blue-black storm clouds that forced us to fly lower and lower, and looking ahead I could now make out a great harbor on the coast, with the dim shapes of several ships anchored in it. Singapore harbor!

Chapter IV

At The Front

We flew low across the harbor. Just before reaching it the Blenheims lowered their wheels to landing position to show they were friendly, so we did likewise, passing over it that way. At the same time, one of the Blenheims shot off a couple of Very lights in a secret color combination to further identify us to the anti-aircraft defenses; we could expect the gunners to be quick on the trigger at a place like this, and we didn't want to get them excited.

I noticed one ship in the harbor that contrasted strangely with the rest, because it was all white except for a narrow green stripe around it and large red crosses on the deck, sides, and funnel. It was the first hospital ship I'd seen, and it looked grimly suggestive there. Little did I suspect that I was to be a passenger on it within a month!

Singapore Island is roughly diamond-shaped, about twenty-five miles long east and west, by fifteen miles north and south, and our destination was Tengah Airdrome on the northwest side. We made it just ahead of a heavy rainstorm that was bearing down from the north, and though the setting sun was still shining from the west, we had to fly through a curtain of rain on the north side when we were approaching to land.

Even circling the drome we could easily see we were in a war zone, for it was spotted with filled-in bomb craters just like the ones in England, and there were quite a few unfilled ones, too, indicating that the airdrome had recently been bombed. There was a fresh hole in one end of the concrete runway that we had to dodge when landing.

After I was down I taxied to a spot as far as possible from any other plane (for dispersal in case of bombing), and hopped out gratefully. As I was stretching to get rid of my cramps, I happened to think that by rights I should have made a ceremony of climbing down from my machine, for it meant that I was setting foot on the continent of Asia for the first time.

I borrowed a screwdriver to remove the panels in the sides and bottom of the fuselage of my airplane, and hurried to untie and unload my baggage, which I had fastened in various nooks and crannies of the framework. A lorry came around to collect some of us, and we were driven to the Officers' Mess, a great beautiful building of dark grey stone at the top of a gentle grassy incline overlooking the airdrome.

There we met the main part of 300 Squadron (my squadron), who had arrived in another group two days before. They had spent the last two days getting their machines into shape and ready for action, and were full of pep because they planned to start operating the next morning. (The group I came in was made up of the remainder of 300 Squadron and some of 175.)

The boys told us they'd had their first taste of Jap bombing the day before, after landing on another airdrome. The place was raided by a formation of twenty-seven bombers at high altitude, and while most of the boys got to cover in time, Mickey, Cam, and Ambrose were caught in the open and just managed to duck into a drainage ditch (fortunately dry), as the bombs were falling. They got showered with dirt from a bomb that landed quite close, but weren't hurt.

I was anxious to get word of my American friend from Waxahachie, Texas, Tex M—, whom I'd said goodbye to in the American Eagle Club just before I left England, when he told me he was going to Singapore. He should have arrived here ahead of us, because we had been delayed and rerouted on the way. Red C—, the Californian in our squadron, who was also a friend of Tex, gave me the bad news. Having arrived here ahead of me in the first group. Red had already inquired, and learned that Tex had been killed a couple of weeks before, shot down in battle with Navy Zeros.

After a supper served by Malay and Chinese waiters in the spacious, airy dining hall of the Officers' Mess, a conference was held in the lounge, between our C.O. and the pilots who were to be on duty next morning. An R.A.F. fighter squadron operates as twelve airplanes, so that not all of the pilots and planes fly each time, and the work is rotated among them. This allows planes to be laid up for servicing and overhauling and provides spares to replace losses, and gives all the pilots an opportunity to rest and provides replacements for their casualties. The twelve who were to operate next day were from the first group to arrive, so that it was as somewhat of an outsider that I sat in on the conference.

Details of formation and tactics were worked out and settled on the basis of what they'd learned about enemy tactics and the capabilities of their airplanes.

They'd received lots of tips and information from other pilots who were fighting the Japs here. The standard enemy raid consisted of twenty-seven bombers flying in close formation at twenty-two thousand feet, escorted by anything up to twenty or thirty Navy Zero fighters flying above them. In attacking these formations it was essential to act fast and try to get at the bombers before the Navy Zeros above could interfere. It was best to attack the bombers either head-on or from the side; very unwise to attack them from the rear, because of the heavy concentration of machine-gun and cannon fire from the rear turrets of all twenty-seven bombers, which focused on anyone coming up from behind.

The enemy usually staged one or two of these raids every forenoon, in addition to little raids and reconnaissance flights at odd hours throughout the rest of the day. We knew that for the time being we must expect to operate against very heavy odds, and that somehow we must try to use enough better tactics and skill to make up the difference.

That night was clear with a full moon, an ideal night for bombing, and there were so many pilots in the Mess that it was decided to disperse us in case the place got hit; so some of us piled into a lorry and were driven to a camp in a rubber estate outside the drome, where we all slept in one big tent.

Once, in the middle of the night, some of us heard a heavy explosion in the distance, and next morning (January 31) we learned what it was. Our armies had been evacuated from the mainland of Malaya, into Singapore Island itself, and a section of the Johore Causeway, a long concrete highway bridge connecting the island with the mainland across the mile-wide Straits of Johore, had been blown up. The enemy armies were now just across these straits, only three or four miles from our airdrome.

That day a B.B.C. news broadcast began with the words, "The Battle of Malaya has ended and the Battle for Singapore has begun!" We had arrived just in time to take part in the defense of an island under siege.

The twelve boys who were to be "on" next morning were up and had breakfast before daylight so as to be on readiness at dawn, while the rest of us got up at our leisure and drifted around to breakfast at about eight o'clock. Even though I wasn't flying that morning I couldn't help feeling some of the tension that I knew the others were undergoing, as they sat around the telephone in their "dispersal huts" at the edge of the field. It was more than three months since any of them had flown in action— and that had been the cautious, sparring sort of game we played back and forth across the Channel with the German fighters through most of 1941. Several had never been in actual combat. Now they were waiting to take off against a new enemy who was all out to crush us, just as the Germans were in the Battle of Britain; so that each time they went up they were quite likely to see combat.

After breakfast we who were off duty lounged about for a time on the veranda overlooking the field, idly watching the scores of coolies, both men and women, at work filling in the bomb craters. Each carried two round wicker baskets, suspended from the ends of a stick across the shoulders. They used little implements like grub hoes to fill the baskets with earth, and then carried their loads to the craters and dumped them.

About nine o'clock someone remarked, "Oh-oh! Looks like the boys have got a scramble."

Sure enough, a frantic bustling was taking place down at the drome. Pilots were bolting from the dispersal huts and racing towards their airplanes, ground crews running to help. Nearest to us, we could see Red take the bottom wing of his machine in a leap and then disappear into his cockpit. A moment of tense quiet followed, while the boys were getting settled in their machines with helmets, parachutes, and seat straps buckled; then, down the line, the first engine came to life, its note rising to a surprised bellow almost as soon as it started, when the pilot slammed his throttle ahead rudely to get going.

Other engines joined the chorus one after another, and clouds of dust billowed up as the Hurricanes left their parking spaces, coolies running in all directions to get out of the way. The field became alive with planes, all heading for the end of the runway, the pilots taxiing jerkily, as fast as they dared, dodging bomb craters, racing in clear stretches, slowing down again, stopping to avoid collisions or let others by, speeding up again, all in a bedlam of noise from the dozen Rolls-Royce engines, each roaring fiercely in spurts, quieting momentarily, bellowing out again, and slowing once more, in response to the hurried manipulations of throttles as the pilots made their way by fits and starts across the drome.

The two leading machines arrived and turned in on the end of the runway, pausing momentarily, their mighty engines trumpeting at idling speed. Then their idling propellers became invisible and a great stentorian roar swept across the field to us, drowning all the other din, as these two machines gathered speed down the runway and were off, skimming up over the boundary, wheels rising upward and inward to their recesses in the fuselages after taking off, like pigeons folding up their legs. Others followed, one pair after another. They made a gentle left-hand climbing sweep around the airdrome, while the last ones to take off caught up and took their places in the formation; then they disappeared into the blue, climbing steeply, and peace and quiet came back to the airdrome.

A few minutes later, the air-raid sirens sounded. No planes were in sight, so we just walked around and located the trenches nearest to the Mess in case we needed to know, then stood outside, waiting for developments and hoping to get our first glimpse of Japanese airplanes.

We were satisfied on the latter score after a few minutes, when three fast single-engined planes, obviously fighters, flew over at about fifteen thousand feet, in loose formation, weaving violently as if they thought they were being chased. They headed away to the north, and one chap who belonged here told us reassuringly, "That's only the reco flight. The bombers will be along in a little while now."

That seemed to be all for the time being, so some of us got a ground crew and a little Farmall tractor, and drove out from the airdrome a mile or so to where a few of our airplanes, including mine, had been parked among some rubber trees for dispersal. There were so many things to be done, like installing radio and oxygen equipment as well as making engine adjustments and thorough checks on each machine before it would be ready to fight, that the ground crews couldn't take care of them all at one time, and some of them were parked out here temporarily.

We hooked the tractor onto one, and after lots of sweating and shoving, finally getting a tow from a passing army truck, we managed to get it out of the woods and up on the road.

About that time we became conscious of a heavy distant drone— not too distant, either— and looking up, we saw an enormous cluster of bombers far above, little close-grouped, silver flecks against the bright blue tropical sky! They were in close formation, just like those we'd heard about— the first mass bombing formation I'd seen since the Battle of Britain, and it held me fascinated.

They were heading to pass to one side of us, so we didn't have to take cover, and we stood in the road watching them, hoping to see our fighters break in among them. However, they started turning, about that time, making a wide sweep and heading away to the north again without dropping their bombs. Apparently they had been warned of the presence of our fighters on patrol and ordered back— something which occurred quite frequently. They seldom followed through with a raid when they knew our fighters were at their altitude in time to meet them. If we could have had earlier warnings of their approach, we should probably have turned back many more raids than we did in the days that followed; but this was impossible now that we had lost Malaya and couldn't keep observers there, for the warnings we usually got didn't give us enough time to reach the altitude of the bombers before they were overhead.

After the formation had gone out of sight we returned to our job, and took the Hurricane back to the airdrome where the crews could work on it. Pretty soon the squadron came back and landed, having been unable to make contact with the enemy; and in a short time they were refuelled and back on readiness.

About eleven o'clock they were scrambled again. I had been chatting with Red in a tool shed near our flight's dispersal hut when the word came. As he dashed out to his airplane I flung a casual "Good luck!" after him, little thinking that I'd have occasion shortly to recall it.

A few minutes after they took off the air raid sirens sounded, but there were no signs of any enemy planes and most of us wandered up to the Mess to pass the time. After a little while we heard "that noise" again— the ominous heavy drone of many distant engines— so we went outdoors, took one look upwards, and then raced for the shelter trenches!

It was another formation of twenty-seven just as before, if not the same one, and this time it was heading to pass right over us. I sat in a trench with my heart pounding from running and excitement, looking up at the cluster of neatly spaced little silvery shapes drawing relentlessly towards us across the sky. Was this their bombing run? It surely looked like it. I rehearsed myself in what to do— crouch down, fingers in ears, mouth wide open, try to avoid touching the sides of the trench— and hope for the best. The next moments were very tense and quiet, all of us subdued, waiting for the warning scream of the bombs.

A battery of heavy anti-aircraft guns opened up near-by with their ear-splitting cracks, and white puffs of smoke began dotting the sky around the formation. It came on steadily until nearly straight above us, and we crouched low, knowing that it would be now if at all.

And then the moment was past and they'd gone over and no bombs had fallen. Relieved, we climbed out of the trenches again, but stayed near at hand, warily, because they might turn around and come back over. I occupied my time carpeting the bottom of my trench with dry leaves, because the ground was damp and sticky and I'd already got my knees muddy.

They didn't come back though, and we watched them flying south and east in the direction of the city until they were out of sight. Then we went back to the Mess, and Ting and I sat out on the veranda, drinking Coca Cola. The air was pleasant, not hot, the sky clear, birds singing in the orchards around the Mess; it might have been a pleasant Sunday morning in summer back home.

We wondered if the squadron would manage to make an interception this time. From the distant sounds it appeared that the bombers were now flying north, up the east side of the island, and as the sound grew more distant we thought we could hear faintly the moan of distant engines power-diving once or twice. We strained our ears for the sound of machine-gun fire which would indicate a fight, but couldn't hear anything more.

After some time a lone Hurricane appeared from the northeast, losing height until it was near the airdrome, when its pilot opened his engine and roared low and fast across the field, rocking his wings in the victory signal. We finished our drinks and hurried down to meet him as he taxied in.

It was Red, and we saw at once that his guns had been fired, because the fabric patches were shot away from the holes in the wings in front of them. He was grinning from ear to ear as he climbed out of his cockpit.

"I got a fighter, Art!" were his first words when he saw me. "Boy, did we have a party!"

Then, after a pause to get control of himself because he was too excited to talk coherently, he went on: "We ran into a whole slew of them at twenty-two thousand feet, somewhere up in Malaya. We'd been chasing all over and hadn't seen a thing, and then all at once we did a turn and there they were, just off on our left, stacks of big twin-engined bombers.

"We sailed right through the formation from one side to the other, shooting at everything in sight. Then when I came out the other side I saw two fighters coming at me— little chubby fellows with great big radial engines in front and painted bright green all over. I thought 'All right, you —s'!' and I started climbing for all I was worth. They couldn't keep up with me at all. I got well above them and then turned and dived on the nearest one. I got real close before I let him have it, and honest, you never saw anything like it. His machine just seemed to explode, with pieces flying off and smoke pouring out. He whipped up sort of, right in front of me, and then spun over sideways. The last I saw of him he was just a ball of fire going down. I gave the other one a burst, too, and I think I damaged him, but I was out of ammunition then so I dived away and headed for home."

By this time Red was the center of a crowd of fellows, all shaking his hand and congratulating him. It was his first combat, and he had realized the good luck we had wished him before he took off.

A Brewster Buffalo fighter came gliding out of the distance, its engine dead. When about three hundred feet up, the pilot apparently saw he couldn't make the drome. He turned and disappeared behind a woods near-by, and the crash truck and ambulance went off in that direction. Later we learned that the pilot had cracked up but wasn't hurt seriously. His engine had been damaged in combat and he'd glided all the way back, trying to make this airdrome and falling only a few hundred yards short.

More Hurricanes were stringing back in at intervals now, until all except four of the boys had landed safely. When these four didn't show up after a reasonable time we began to get worried. Finally we got a call from Sembawang Airdrome, a few miles to the east, informing us that three of the four missing boys had force-landed there with their airplanes shot up, and were unhurt. They were Kleck (the American from Florida), Denny, and Mickey. The C.O. drove over to get them, returning about mid-afternoon, and after razzing them for "forgetting to duck" we listened to their stories.

Denny had shot down a bomber in flames, making the morning's score two definitely destroyed, in addition to several damaged. He had got some bullets in his engine and radiator from return fire from the bombers, so that his oil tank and radiator went dry and his engine overheated and "seized," on the way back. He just made Sembawang, which was the nearest airdrome.

Kleck, the Florida boy, also had an exciting time. He damaged a couple of bombers in the initial attack and then turned around to chase after one that was lagging behind the rest. He was almost within range when a Navy Zero fighter jumped him from behind. The first thing he knew, showers of tracers were going by him and there were several loud explosions in his airplane from cannon shells. Then he was blinded by steam and glycol and oil spray in his cockpit, so he rolled over and dived to get away. Flames were coming from his engine and he thought he would have to jump; but the fire went out after a moment and being over enemy territory he chose to try to make it home. His engine ran intermittently, giving him a little power, although catching fire a couple of times more for short periods. He finally made it to the Straits and across them to Sembawang. The field was badly bombed, with many unfilled craters. As he didn't have enough height to glide in on the runway, he had to land right among some craters. He bounced over most of them and then rolled to a stop at the edge of one, miraculously avoiding a crackup.

Mickey said he "had a go" at one bomber and was attacking another when he suddenly noticed "funny little holes," as he described them, appearing around him in his machine, whereupon he dived away. His engine and radiator were hit so that he, too, was blinded by steam, glycol, and oil. Once he thought he was on fire and unfastened his straps with the intention of bailing out, but the fire didn't materialize. Then he saw Sembawang ahead so he stayed with his machine, trying to make it. When he got there his windshield was so covered with oil and glycol that he couldn't see enough to tell whether he was landing on the runway or not, and like Kleck he landed among the bomb craters. This was very bad, because he hadn't had a chance to fasten his straps again— the straps keep you from being thrown forward in a crash, so you're not so likely to be injured. When Mickey saw the bomb craters going past his wings he retracted his wheels so that his machine dropped down on its belly and slid to a quick stop— a very wise move. By thus deliberately doing a minor crash he avoided the probability of a serious one, for if left on its wheels his plane would probably have rolled on until it hit a bomb crater. Not expecting to see anyone there whom he knew, he was quite astounded, on climbing out of his wrecked machine, to see Denny and Kleck approaching, laughing at him; and to learn that he was the third to force-land there!

Only one pilot now remained missing. That was Bruce, a New Zealand boy, one of the finest chaps I've known and the best-liked boy in the squadron. He hasn't been heard of since, and I believe he is now listed as "missing, believed killed." Though we knew we had to expect casualties now, we felt it was too bad that he, of all of us, had to be the first.

There was a Chinese business man in Singapore who had a standing offer of a bottle of champagne for every Jap plane destroyed, so that evening Red and Denny, accompanied by some of the others, drove into town to collect the two bottles they had earned by their victories.

Those of us who hadn't flown that day were to take over on the morrow, so I went to bed with high hopes of having my first crack at the Japs in the morning.

Chapter V

Island Under Siege

I had taken over a nice airy room in the Mess that day, and once during the night I awoke at the sound of air-raid sirens. A little later, dreamily, I heard the noise of anti-aircraft guns, of two or three airplanes droning about in the distance, and then the far-away thuds of several bombs exploding.

Next morning when I got up I saw a new landmark to the east which was to remain part of the scenery for as long as I stayed in Singapore. The bombers in the night had hit and set fire to one of the great oil storage tanks near the naval base a few miles east of us. The landmark was a great sinister column of black smoke, with red flames at its bottom, rising and widening Vesuvius-like to a height of three or four thousand feet where it flattened out and stretched southward in a long dark ugly mantle as far as we could see.

I didn't get to fly that day either. My high hopes of seeing my first action against the Japs were frustrated by a new and most disappointing order which we received early in the morning. Our squadron were to leave Singapore and move to Palembang, a Dutch city three hundred miles south in Sumatra, not far from the jungle airdrome where we stopped on our way up here. We were to go there because the prospect of enemy raids on Palembang and on shipping in the Banka Straits nearby had made it necessary for a squadron to be stationed in the vicinity.

We were all terribly disappointed. None of us wanted to go, for here in Singapore we were right in the middle of things, while it would be comparatively quiet, so we thought, in Sumatra. And so it was that I felt anything but sorry when the C.O. told me I was to remain here temporarily at least, in charge of a group of the boys who were being left behind. It was necessary to leave six behind because there were that many airplanes not serviceable for the trip — the three which had been damaged in the fight the day before and had force-landed at Sembawang, and three others that had minor troubles or damage.

The only order the C.O. gave me was to do what I could toward getting these machines into flying condition — though I'm quite sure he knew I'd have my own ideas about what to do with them after that!

The boys took off for Palembang after lunch, leaving the airdrome strangely empty and silent after the roar of their engines had died away in the distance. Ours had been the only squadron here at Tengah, 175 Squadron having taken up residence at Seletar Airdrome on the east side of the island. The countryside was quiet, the afternoon sunny and pleasant. The only sign of war was the silent, sullen black smoke column brooding above the horizon east and south of us. I found it hard to realize that we were besieged by a great army, just across a narrow strip of water no wider than the Mississippi River!

I had inherited for my use a beautiful new 1942 Ford sedan which the C.O. had been provided with; but Kleck, who was one of the group staying with me, wasn't to be outdone. He appeared later in the afternoon, triumphantly driving a '41 Chewy he had promoted; it had been left behind by a bomber pilot whose unit was unexpectedly moved away!

We were able to use these cars to good advantage during the next couple of days, at the task of getting our airplanes repaired. Normally a squadron's ground personnel look after all repair work, but in this case our ground personnel weren't available. They had come only as far as Sumatra and would probably remain there, along with the squadron's equipment and spares. We were little better than orphans here.

We had the cooperation of another unit, who supplied us with a crew of men to work on our machines, and helped us in other ways, and we drove all over the island, visiting various places to procure needed spare parts and tools. This was a highly interesting way of passing the time until we could start flying again, for it gave us a chance to see what the island was like. We got a radiator here, a wingtip there, a couple of propellers from different sources, a propeller installation tool kit from another place, and so on. We made frequent trips to Sembawang, of course, taking spares for the three machines which Kleck, Denny, and Mickey had landed there, and checking on the repair work.

Most of the island seemed to be wooded, either jungle or rubber plantations. Vegetation was rich and green everywhere, due, I suppose, to the large rainfall. The soil itself didn't look rich, being mostly a sort of light brown clay. The roads were good, mostly blacktop, and wound pleasantly through forests, rubber estates, and curious little Malayan-Chinese villages. It was here that I finally became completely at home driving on the wrong side of the road, for the traffic was left-hand as in England, all the cars, of course, having the driver's seat on the right.

The Japs weren't to launch their actual assault against the island for several days more, and most of the time it was fairly quiet except for an air raid or two each day. I spent quite a bit of time working on airplanes at the drome at Tengah, and occasionally had to leave my work to take cover at sight of enemy planes.

On one occasion I really had to run for it. I was putting a wingtip on a machine, working alone, and was so engrossed that I failed to notice the drone of an approaching bomber formation until I had been listening to it for perhaps three or four minutes. Suddenly coming to, I looked up to see them almost overhead, a standard high altitude raid. The nearest shelter trenches were a couple of hundred yards away, so I jumped into my car, parked beside the airplane, and started off with my wheels spinning.

As I approached the trenches I could see some Indian Army soldiers diving into them, so I knew I'd split the timing pretty close and just yanked the emergency brake handle and landed running, without waiting for the car to stop. The bombers were directly overhead. I dived into a trench with a couple of Indian Sikhs and crouched down, waiting; but the bombers passed on and no bombs fell, so I climbed out again.

The heavy anti-aircraft guns were barking furiously. All at once I heard a whistling noise as of a bomb falling, and in practically one leap I landed on my knees in the trench, in a huddle with the Sikhs again. There was no explosion, so after a minute or so we cautiously stuck our heads above ground, looked warily all around like so many gophers leaving their holes, and then climbed out.

I found I had muddied my arms and legs and cut one knee in this second leap for cover, so I drove back to the Mess to clean up. There I found Kleck in almost identical condition, his arms and legs muddied and one knee cut also. It seemed that he had heard that same noise and leaped back into the trench he'd been using, just as I did, with the same result. We made quite a joke out of being "wounded" in a bombless air raid! We didn't know what made the whistling sound that scared us, but presumed it was a dud anti-aircraft shell, falling back to earth after failing to explode in the air.

They never did bomb Tengah Airdrome while we were there, in spite of passing over it frequently. Either they went on to bomb somewhere else or turned away at the approach of our fighters. Once we saw them bomb Sembawang Airdrome several miles away— an impressive sight. We couldn't see the drome itself from Tengah, but we saw the scores of smoke clouds shooting up in a quick procession across that section of our horizon, tumbling and swirling together to a height of perhaps three or four hundred feet. The sound came to us— awe-inspiring, heavy sustained booming and rumbling that lasted for several seconds while the earth under us shook and trembled from the distant explosions. Gradually the smoke clouds rose and thinned away, leaving only a couple of small black columns from fires that were started.

In the Officers' Mess the Malay waiters and batmen had all run off after the news that the enemy were so near, but the two elderly Chinese cooks and "Tichi," a little Malay boy of ten or eleven who worked in the bar, remained on the job. The meals were still lavish, the only difference being that we had to serve ourselves. There was always plenty of ice-cold beer, as well as Coca Cola and other soft drinks, to be had.

We had a pleasant surprise on the third or fourth day after the squadron had gone to Palembang, when they all returned, roaring out of the south late in the afternoon and swooping low across the airdrome to let us know they'd arrived. After they landed we learned that they'd come up to escort a bombing raid on an enemy position in Malaya at dawn next morning, and I promised the C.O. I'd have three of my machines ready to go with them on the raid.

The boys' opinion of Sumatra hadn't improved during the time they were there, and they were all glad to get back and wished they could stay. There had been almost nothing for them to do in the line of flying, except some monotonous convoy patrols. The closest any of them had come to action was an occasional chase after lone bombers, snooping around ships in the Banka Straits, that ducked away into clouds at sight of their Hurricanes. They said it was hotter than before, the bugs, snakes, and lizards all doing well and thicker than ever, and the mosquitoes still growing.

I had to work a good share of that night with my crews, finishing repair jobs and doing final inspections on the three machines that I'd promised the C.O. I'd have ready. It was bright moonlight, and we worked and sweated and toiled until about two o'clock in the morning. Then with the last engine checked, the last fuel tank filled, the last gun cleaned and loaded, and the last cowling clip fastened I told the men they could go to bed and take the morning off. Then I drove wearily back to the Mess for two or three hours' sleep myself before the raid. I was to take part in it, so naturally I was looking forward once more to getting my first action against the Japs.

It was all in vain though. A change in the situation at dawn made it necessary to cancel the whole raid, and about midmorning the squadron were ordered to fly back to Palembang.

I was again to stay behind, but three of my pilots were to go with the squadron, taking the three airplanes that we had got ready. I tried to talk the C.O. out of taking these airplanes. It hurt our pride to see bombers coming over each day and not be able to do anything about it except run for shelter and then watch from our trenches. I had hoped that I could get started operating with my bunch and get a crack at them. But the C.O. said he was afraid he might need the airplanes at Palembang. He consoled me by saying that if I got any more planes in serviceable condition I could keep them and use them, for the time being at least.

Kleck was one of the three of my group who had to go to Palembang with the squadron this time, and he was quite put out about it. He had the same hopes I had about operating here, and he naturally didn't think he'd get any action down there in Sumatra.

He shouldn't have worried on that score. He was destined to get more action there than I got in Singapore, and I was never to see him again.

That would have left only three pilots in my group, but after the squadron left I saw that two of the machines hadn't taken off with the rest. The pilots were Denny and Sergeant H——. They both had engine trouble and would have to wait over for a day or two. So for the moment there were five of us. Denny was a flight commander in the squadron and senior to me, so he automatically was in charge of our group.

By this time we were beginning to hear a little more of the noises of war. Particularly at night we could hear distant guns booming out an occasional few rounds. We expected that as the enemy got time to bring more of their artillery into position we'd be hearing much more. Our airdrome was only two or three miles from the edge of the narrow straits separating us from the enemy.

Towards noon of the day after our squadron flew back to Palembang we were all surprised by a visit from 175 Squadron (whose pilots came out to Singapore with us). As I mentioned before, they had been operating from Seletar Airdrome on the northeast side of the island, right on the edge of the Straits. They had been forced to take off on very short notice this morning and fly over here, when the enemy began shelling their drome!

We were all glad to see one another and had quite a reunion in the Mess, swapping accounts of what we'd been doing. They said they'd had lots of patrols and chases and had fought two or three engagements with moderate success.

It was about noon and we were all lounging on the veranda, swapping stories and waiting for lunch to be ready, when suddenly the quiet was broken by a muffled explosion, a whistling noise, and then a loud explosion, all in rapid order:

"Whoompf— phe-ew — *BLAM*!"

The building shook a little. Conversation stopped in midair. We exchanged glances, and I looked around for a place to duck.

Someone ventured, "I didn't hear any airplane!"

"Whoompf— phe-ew— *BLAM*!" The building shook again.

Someone else said, "That isn't a plane!"

Then a startled "Look!" and there on the far side of the airdrome we saw two thin flat clouds of light blue smoke drifting along just above the ground, about fifty yards apart. As we looked, there was a bright flash in the ground near them and the earth shot upwards and outward in a cloud of dust and smoke. The same noise came to us a second later. We all knew what it was now without being told. The time had come for what was to be my first of five evacuations under fire in two weeks. Our airdrome, too, was being shelled!

The barrage lasted over an hour, but nothing landed nearer the Mess than a hundred yards or so; and most of us ate our lunches unperturbed. We weren't going to let them spoil our last meal here, anyhow.

Joe H—, one of 175's pilots who was delayed taking off and didn't leave Seletar until some time after the rest, came into the dining hall while we were eating. He looked quite shaken— and with reason. Just as he was levelling off to land on the runway two shells had exploded, one on either side of him, throwing his machine partly out of control and nearly causing him to crash!

Through the windows of the Mess we saw a low thatched-roof wooden building on the far side of the drome catch fire and begin burning hotly. A Brewster Buffalo landed, and as it was taxiing to the edge of the field a shell crashed beside it, turning it upside down and injuring the pilot. Someone took my car to drive him to the dressing station. When I got it back I had to clean blood off the seat and dashboard.

The barrage ceased after an hour or so, for no apparent reason— probably because the enemy thought it was enough to show us we couldn't use the drome and because they didn't want to damage it any more in case they were able to use it later themselves.

From the Far East Command Communique

Singapore, February 5. There has been some enemy shelling in the north of the island, with negligible results. Air reports show much enemy movement southward in Johore. Enemy aircraft have continued to make high-level and low dive-bombing and machine-gun attacks on the island, causing comparatively little damage or casualties.

Shipping in the harbor was also attacked. An oil tanker at the naval base, which was set on fire two days ago by enemy bombing, is still burning.

Hurricane fighters of the R.A.F. intercepted a large formation of enemy aircraft over Singapore this morning. One enemy aircraft was destroyed, one probably destroyed, and one damaged by our aircraft.

Chapter VI

Into the Fight

With the airdromes of Tengah and Seletar under shellfire and Sembawang vulnerable to it at any time (for it was right on the edge of the Straits), there was only one place left from which we could operate. This was Kallang Airdrome, the former municipal airport of Singapore, on the south side of the island just east of the city.

175 Squadron were now ordered to move down there, and we did likewise, taking our two Hurricanes and two automobiles. The engine troubles on the Hurricanes had been remedied, but the weather was reported bad in the direction of Sumatra so that the pilots, Denny and Sergeant H—, couldn't go to Palembang yet to rejoin the Squadron.

They flew the Hurricanes across to Kallang while I drove my Ford, and Brownie and Ted took the Chewy which Kleck had promoted. We of course loaded our baggage into the two cars before leaving; in addition, I brought along a bag of things belonging to Bruce, the boy who went missing from the squadron's first engagement. I wanted to have it sent back to his folks.

Driving to Kallang I had to pass through the city of Singapore, my first visit to it. I took time off to drive around a little, looking at the sights, and then headed out east of town to the airdrome.

This was a sorry sight if there ever was one. The road entering the airdrome passed under imposing dark stone archways, now pitifully scarred and chipped by blast and shrapnel and bullets. The beautiful hangars and terminal buildings of what had once been a great airline base were barren and empty, with windows gone, walls gashed and torn. It reminded me of the buildings at Croydon Airdrome, London's great airline terminal, as they look today — deserted, because there are no airlines, with ticket and information booths silent and empty, their counters covered with dust, windows blown in and walls shattered and scarred, results of the great mass bombing raid Croydon received in August 1940.

The vast concrete aprons between and in front of the hangars here were torn and pitted with bomb craters, as was the entire field.

The saddest sight of all was the remains of several Hurricanes and Brewsters, as well as three or four trucks and tank wagons, around the outside of the field — sorry-looking, smashed and twisted wreckages, mostly burned out, the victims of bombing and machine-gun attacks. It was heart-breaking.

The Hurricanes had already arrived from Tengah and were now dispersed around the field with mechanics working on them, giving them their "D/I's," or daily inspections. Denny was gone, so I inquired for directions to the Officers' Mess and found it a couple of miles from the drome.

But there were only smoldering ruins at the spot. The Mess had been hit and set on fire by bombs the day before, and was completely burned out. I found Denny and some of the others there, salvaging the bar stock from a refrigerator in the ruins— bottles of beer and liquor.

We didn't know it yet, but Squadron Leader L—, the C.O. of 175 Squadron, was acting fast in this little emergency. By evening he had arranged for all of us to be put up in the exclusive Sea View Hotel on the seashore several miles east of town, which was supposed to be one of the most luxurious places in Singapore. I found myself ensconced in a room which was like a movie star's boudoir in its furnishings — elaborate wardrobes, tables, dressers, cabinets — all in beautiful hardwood; expensive-looking chairs, settees (I think you call them), stools, footstools, and perhaps as many as half a dozen mirrors. I had little trouble, as you can guess, in finding room for my wardrobe of shirt and shorts when I climbed into the huge, luxurious bed. A couple of days later I learned that a small but nicely furnished sitting room adjacent belonged with my room. Altogether, it was a strange lair from which to go forth to battle.

One side of the hotel looked out on the sea, but the main entrance was in the crook of an "L" formed by the building, and faced away from the sea onto a pretty little lawn filled with palm trees, its beauty somewhat spoiled by shelter trenches dug in it. There were several automobiles — including ours — scattered about there, too, because patrons were required to park their cars under the trees for concealment.

Dinner that evening was seven courses, served by Chinese and Malay waiters in a spacious dining hall where we saw lots of wealthy civilians, including the first white women we'd seen in some time, wearing the first evening dresses we'd seen in months.

After dinner Denny and I talked things over, discussing what we should do now. He was as anxious to remain in Singapore as I was. Technically we were under the orders of our C.O., but he was three hundred miles away in Palembang and would naturally expect us to use our own initiative in what we did, now that circumstances were changing so fast.

Our most obvious course, one which didn't appeal to us, was to follow the squadron to Palembang, two of us flying in the two Hurricanes and the other three going by the first available boat. We not only hated to go back there, where (we thought) things would be very quiet, but also we sincerely felt that we and our airplanes would be more useful here during the crucial days ahead.

175 Squadron had been working hard ever since they arrived, and the pilots were getting tired. Also they were getting short of airplanes, so that they could use our two to good advantage. Reinforcements of either pilots or planes would be hard to get now. They were a swell crowd of fellows and we knew them so well from having been together on the voyage out that we'd just as soon fight with

them as with our own bunch. Denny finally decided that we would offer to help them.

Next morning after breakfast he spoke to Squadron Leader L—, the squadron's C.O., offering to put ourselves and our two airplanes at his disposal if Air Headquarters would O.K. it. Squadron Leader L— was delighted with the idea. He rang up Air Headquarters and gave them such a convincing sales talk over the phone that in a matter of minutes the plan was O.K.'d and we were officially "attached" to 175 Squadron. We also pooled our two cars with those which the squadron already had, with the result that the squadron was well off for pilots' transportation from then on. Now at last, I thought, I should surely be getting my much-delayed action against the Japs.

We all had some business and shopping we wanted to take care of, so Denny asked our new C.O. if we could have a couple of hours off to run into town before we went to work. The C.O. insisted that we should take the whole day off and not start flying until the next day.

Accordingly, four of us — Denny, Ted, Brownie, and I — piled into the Ford and drove to town to tend to our business and capitalize on our first chance to spend some time in the city and see what it was like.

The business section seemed to be very modern, and it might have been an American city except for the welter of Chinese and Malays all about and the rickshas mingling with modern cars on the streets. However, we soon tired and lost interest in sight-seeing as it was a very hot day, and stopped for refreshments at the Raffles Hotel, supposed to be one of the popular hot-spots of the town. There we saw an advertisement for the film "Ziegfeld Girl" at the Alhambra Theatre near-by; we voted for a matinee of that in preference to further sight-seeing, until the heat of the day was past.

The theatre was small, with a pleasant interior that belied a rather shabby outside appearance. The air-raid sirens sounded shortly after the picture started, and Ted and Brownie, who had steel helmets, clapped them on until the all clear sounded a while later.

It perhaps wasn't just the show we would have chosen if we had had a choice, for though the music and lavish pageants were wonderful, the sight of so many beautiful girls was almost more than we could take after being away from feminine companionship for so long! The shock was quite rude for us when it was over; completely lost in the lovely atmosphere of American girls and song and gaiety and peace, we stepped outside into the teeming oriental traffic and the sweltering tropical sun, to be reminded that we were half-way around the world from America, with our enemies only a few miles away.

Towards mid-afternoon we returned to the hotel; there we learned to our very keen sorrow that our new C.O., Squadron Leader L—, had been killed while we were downtown.

He was a fine C.O., loved by all his boys, and we ourselves had known him well enough to like him very much also. Two of the other boys had been shot down but escaped injury, although their machines were wrecked.

One of the boys shot down, Joe H—, was first to tell us about Squadron Leader L—'s death. Joe himself had had a very narrow escape. He'd had his machine badly shot up by Navy Zeros and had to run for it, racing low over the sea to get away from two of them, his damaged engine running wide open with its radiator shot through and running dry, with the result that just after he got clear of them his engine "seized" and he had to force-land near the shore of an island. His Hurricane was almost torn to pieces by rocks just beneath the surface of the water, but luckily it stayed right side up and he managed to get out safely. He was picked up by a motor launch whose crew saw him land, and they brought him into Singapore harbor, where he got a ride by car to the hotel. We found him resting there when we arrived, a very shaken boy. It was he who had had the narrow escape the day before when two shells nearly wrecked him as he was landing at Tengah.

Later in the afternoon we drove from the hotel out to the airdrome to see what was going on, and there I met an old friend of mine, a New Zealand pilot, who had been stationed at the airdrome near London where I was, a year or so before.

He said he had been out in Singapore since before the fighting started, and as flight commander in a squadron of Brewster Buffaloes he had been in nearly all the fighting which went on here. He was so worn and haggard and had lost so much weight that I hardly recognized him. He said he had just been promoted to squadron leader and was going down to Java to re-form his squadron, as most of their planes had been lost and most of their pilots killed. He himself was off flying for at least a week or two because of shock from a bomb that had landed too close to him a few days before.

I advised him to try to get sent away for a rest, even if it meant losing his promotion temporarily. He looked much too tired and ill to carry on long.

With Squadron Leader L—'s death, Rickey, one of the flight commanders, became C.O. of the squadron, and Denny was made flight commander in his place. Three airplanes had been lost during the day but only one pilot, so that with the addition of us five pilots from 300 Squadron there were now twice as many pilots as planes. That meant that each of the two flights (into which any squadron is divided) had enough pilots to man all the airplanes. Rickey therefore instituted a program whereby the two flights changed off, one bunch doing all the work while the other rested.

Because the heavy attacks usually came about midmorning, Rickey instituted a short shift from 9:00 a.m. to 1:00 p.m. for one flight to do, to take care of these heavy raids; the other flight would be on duty the rest of the daylight hours both before and after this shift.

I was in Denny's flight and we were scheduled to do the short shift next morning, so we didn't have to get up very early. After we finished our five-course breakfasts we all sat around on the covered veranda at the entrance to the hotel, reading the morning papers and gossiping, for we still had an hour or so to kill before time to go out to the airdrome.

The distant drone of Rolls-Royce engines in the sky reached our ears, telling us that the other flight had already gone up on patrol; for the first time in more than three months I began to experience the familiar tension and nervousness, with the sickish pain in the pit of my stomach unusually strong. I suppose it was the realization coming home that I was "in it" once more, with all the uncertainties and dismaying possibilities to get used to and subdue again into their places as normal parts of life.

Denny and I spent a little time talking over the formation we'd use and discussing the tactics we would try to employ. Because of our small number of airplanes. Air Headquarters had ordered us to operate as a squadron of eight until we got more reinforcements, to give us a better percentage in reserve. Accordingly, we planned to fly in two sections of four, Denny leading one section and I the other. If we engaged a bombing raid escorted by fighters — the usual thing — I would endeavor to engage the fighters with my four to keep them diverted while Denny took his section into the bombers. Then the next time we'd change around, and he'd do the dirty work with his four while I went for the bombers.

As we talked and I visualized the situations we were discussing, I found my excitement increasing until my heart was pounding and my knees trembled a little — and after eighteen months of mainly front-line service, too!

It seemed so strange to be there relaxing, or trying to, in the cool quiet veranda of the hotel, nonchalantly discussing how we should go about the bizarre and unearthly business that might occur in that other eerie world miles above us before the morning was out, while ordinary civilian men and women lounged around us, finishing their coffee, reading the morning papers, chatting as ordinary people anywhere might, not planning to kill anyone — their greatest danger a probable sea voyage to Java in a few days. I had my helmet, gloves, and mae west in my lap, having just unpacked them from my things, and their significance helped to make it all seem too incongruous to be real!

The other six pilots of our flight were sitting near-by, and presently Denny looked at his watch and announced: "Eight-fifteen. I reckon we might as well get on down there."

We strolled out to where the Ford was parked among the palm trees on the lawn, and the eight of us piled in. I was wondering how long it would take me to get over feeling like a little boy on his first day at school.

As we were backing out from under the palm trees we heard the Hurricanes roar low overhead going towards the drome, so we knew the boys had finished their patrol. We could see them circling to land as we drove along, and by the time we reached the drome they had all landed and taxied to their places along the edge of the field. The pilots were heading toward the dispersal hut when we got there (we had just one hut for all of us at Kallang), and when they saw us piling out of the car they began taking off their mae wests and tossing them gratefully aside.

Denny looked over the list of available machines and assigned them to us while we were putting on our mae wests and otherwise getting ready. I changed from my shorts to a pair of slacks that I kept for flying in action (for protection to my legs in case of fire). Others had overalls; some flew with no extra protection.

I shouldered my parachute and went out to get my airplane ready. The crews were just finishing refuelling it and checking it over after its last patrol. I thought, "Ten minutes to get ready, and then any time after that," and my heart went to pounding again.

There were a number of minor things to take care of in getting my Hurricane to readiness. Because my legs aren't long enough for me to climb into the cockpit of a Hurricane easily when wearing a parachute, I placed my parachute in the seat, so I could put it on after getting in— laying out its straps and the seat straps in neat order so I could reach them quickly without getting them twisted. Then I hung my helmet over the gunsight behind my windshield and plugged the radio lead and oxygen tube into their connections in the side of the cockpit. My gloves I tucked between the gunsight and the windshield. There were checks to make on oxygen supply, air pressure system, and the electric gunsight. There were other minor little odds and ends to do that would each save a second in starting— like turning the gasoline on, unscrewing the primer pump so it was ready for use, turning on the ignition switches, and setting the throttle just right for starting. Because the field was soft and muddy I pumped my wing flaps down a little to assist in getting off the ground quickly; and of course, being built rather small, I checked the position of my seat and raised it as high as it could be set.

Finally satisfied that I had everything ready I made my way back to the dispersal hut and joined the rest of the boys, who were sitting in easy chairs on the porch, waiting. My feelings seemed pretty well under control again, and I realized that I was slipping quite rapidly into my old mental Attitude — combining fighting fever and resignation to "come what may." That is my best means of keeping my fears under control while in action.

I could see by the faces of some of the 175 Squadron boys around me that the strain of constant flying and fighting for the past several days was beginning to tell. Our orders to scramble would come by telephone, and each time the phone rang they'd start nervously and lean forward tensely, until the orderly who answered it told us what the call was about. It rang every three or four minutes, but each call for the first half hour was just some inconsequential message, such as someone wanting to speak to one of the mechanics or an officer wanting to speak to the armorer sergeant— and they'd all relax again.

It reminded me of Battle of Britain days in 1940, when my squadron did their readiness in a tent at Hawkinge Airdrome on the southeast coast of England; we all used to start in the same way with our hearts pounding each time the phone rang — often to learn that it was only some aircraftman reporting that he'd missed the bus back from lunch — and would we please send it back for him! After that we'd all sit back again, sighing deeply, each feeling that he'd been done out of another week's growth. Some psychologist should try to work out a different kind of alarm that would be less agonizing to taut nerves than that quick, jarring ring which becomes almost nightmarish in times of heavy strain.

After we'd been at readiness for some time we heard the orderly taking a call and this time, after listening a moment, he replied to the voice at the other end, "Twenty thousand? Yes, sir."

Someone said, "That's it!" and there was a shuffling and scraping of chairs as we started getting to our feet. The orderly turned to us from the phone to repeat what he was told: "Thirty plus bandits, above twenty thousand feet, approaching from the northwest. Scramble and gain altitude as fast as possible!"

I found myself sprinting towards my machine, which was near-by, heard a Ford V-8 starting up and getting away fast, tires spinning as it careened past me — my own Ford, with pilots hanging on the running boards — the boys whose machines were farthest away using it to save a few seconds.

The alert ground crews were already starting our engines. Mine was running and the mechanic climbing out of the cockpit when I got there, and I scrambled in. There was the old feverish fumbling at parachute and seat straps, helmet and gloves— the glancing around to see if I was late and whether the others were taxiing out yet.

All tucked in and ready to go at last, I found my tenseness relaxing its hold a little. A moment's wait with engine idling, for Denny's four machines to taxi out ahead, and then I was following after them onto the rain-soaked field, fast but carefully, dodging the newly filled bomb craters in which the earth would still be soft. It wasn't safe to take off in formation, because of the condition of the field, but Denny's four followed one another off quickly and I timed my taxiing to arrive in position just after them, with the rest of my section coming along behind me.

Denny was already a distant little silhouette up ahead, climbing and turning, over the harbor; the other three of his section following, with the last one just leaving the ground, when I opened my throttle. There was the raucous full-throated bellowing of my own thousand-horsepower engine, the hurricane windstream forming a wall around the cockpit, tugging at my helmet and blasting my face when I peered out to watch for bad spots in the field; then came the surge of the airplane picking up speed fast, the growing tightness and responsiveness of the controls, and I was off and skimming up over the boundary, shoving my hydraulic control to wheels up, drawing back throttle and propeller pitch controls to ease the engine. A red light showed in my instrument panel, indicating that my wheels were clear up in their retracted position. I shoved the hydraulic control over to flaps up and felt my machine sag a little as its flaps came up from their downward position so that their lifting effect was lost; I began to gain speed faster, the result of lowered wind resistance with the wheels and flaps out of the way.

Ahead of me I could see the silhouettes of Denny's four machines, climbing fast in a gentle left turn and "forming up" together in their assigned order. Below, the blue-green sea of Singapore's outer harbor was slowly curving backward beneath my wings and receding away.

I was in a left turn, too, cutting it shorter than Denny in order to catch him. Behind me the three other planes of my section were trailing, gradually overtaking me and drawing up into their places. My "number two" was fifty or sixty yards off on my right and a little behind; my "numbers three and four" were staggered off on my left and about the same distances apart. Overtaking Denny's section we throttled back and took up position two or three hundred yards away to his left and a little back. It was just a loose easy "search" formation, in which we could guard each other against surprise attacks, and in which we could either act independently as two units or close in and work together, as circumstances dictated.

The crackling of the radio in my ears was broken intermittently by the whirr of transmitters as various conversations were carried on.

Denny's voice came through, calling Control. "Hello, Rastus; hello, Rastus! Tiger Leader calling. Have you any fresh information on the bandits? Over."

A second later the distant controller's voice came back in reply: "Hello, Tiger Leader, Tiger Leader! Rastus answering. Thirty plus bandits now twenty miles northwest of island, above twenty thousand feet, still coming this way. Over!"

We climbed furiously, whipping our engines hard, the noses of our airplanes pointed steeply upward, reaching up and up toward that strange world of thin cold air above us. Denny was leading us wisely in a long sweep out over the sea south of the island, where we could be "upsun" of our enemies.

"Hello, Green One. Green Two calling. One of your wheels is down a little. Over."

Green One and Green Two were the two pilots on the left of me in my section, and glancing over at the nearest of them I saw the outline of one of his wheels halfway down out of its recess in the bottom of the fuselage. Then it disappeared up into place.

Brownie was Green One. His voice came over the R/T (radio telephone) now. "Thank you. Green Two. Is it O.K. now?"

"Yes, it's O.K. now. Green One."

We roared onward and upward, the sun growing brighter and the air clearer. At ten thousand feet it was getting chilly, so I slid my transparent cockpit hood forward, closed, and the cockpit was suddenly quiet with most of the racket and the wind shut out and the noise of the engine reduced to a heavy drone.

Singapore Island was now a miniature in brilliant tropical green far below, landscaped with miniature jungles, orchards, fields, roads, villages, and towns, with the miniature city and harbor on its south coast, all partially screened by a layer of low broken clouds sprinkled over it like hundreds of tufts of white cotton fluff, pretty in the bright sunlight.

It was dwarfed by the green expanses of the great Malayan Peninsula which half swallows it in the hollow of its southern tip into which the island fits, and by the endless reaches of warm blue-green sea stretching in all other directions. Over it ran the long dark mantle of smoke from the oil fire, stretching from its source on the north side, down across and southward out over the sea into the southern horizon.

My altimeter reached the fifteen-thousand-foot mark, and about that time I pulled the control which "changes gears" on the engine's two-speed supercharger so it will give better power at high altitude, and also opened the oxygen regulator valve on my instrument panel to start it feeding oxygen into my face mask. We kept climbing hard, still out over the sea a way, in a gentle left-hand sweep.

Control came on again. "The bandits are just north of the island now, altitude twenty-two thousand or above."

It didn't sound so good. We'd be very lucky if we could reach their altitude by the time they were over the island. Starting a fight with a disadvantage in altitude is one of the most reliable ways of committing suicide. Denny seemed unperturbed, and continued the sweep. He knew there was no use going in to meet them until we had enough height.

Finally when our altimeters read twenty thousand he turned and led us in toward the island, still climbing hard, chancing that we could gain enough altitude before we met them. It would have been much better could we have waited until we had twenty-five thousand feet or so, for then we could come in with a definite advantage in height; but there just wasn't time enough for that. As it was, we still had another two thousand feet to gain just to reach the height of the bombers. If my section were to engage the fighters, which would be above them, we needed considerably more altitude than that or we might have a bad time. But there was no choice.

We came in over the city, still climbing hard. Twenty-one thousand feet now, still another thousand to gain at the very least. Control came on again. "The bandits are over the northwest part of the island now, flying south, still at twenty-two thousand and above."

Denny had us climbing so steeply that my air-speed indicator showed less than one hundred and twenty miles an hour of forward speed, and my controls felt sloppy, as if my airplane were nearing a stall. I'd turned on my gun sight and switched the safety ring around my firing button to the "FIRE" position long since.

We turned left and headed westward, hoping to cut them off. Our formation was getting very ragged. It's hard to keep good formation in the thin air at high altitudes in which the airplanes tend to wallow around loosely, and now every pilot was tense, watching all around for first signs of the enemy, not paying much attention to formation-keeping.

I noticed that one of the machines in Denny's section which had been lagging behind the rest had now disappeared entirely. Engine trouble, I presumed. That left only seven of us.

Twenty-two thousand feet at last, and we were over the southeast part of the island with still no enemies in sight. Denny led us in a left turn, until we were heading south.

For all my keenness to get into battle, the cry, when it came, jolted me.

"Bandits to the left— tally-ho!"

We wheeled into a steep left turn at the cry, and I saw them, in the distance to my dismay, a weird cluster of silver insects sticking out starkly against the blue, heading away from us toward the city. I felt like crying as I realized the situation, for somehow they had got around past us while we were trying to head them off. Now we would have to chase them, and they already had a good start.

It was a weird chase. At that height you hardly seem to be moving, even at three hundred miles an hour or more. We seemed to just hover there while our engines screamed and bellowed, "flat out," boring away at the thin air, trying to overtake the enemy formation which we could see poised against the sky ahead of us like a surrealist painting, with above them the tiny silhouettes of several fighters wheeling about. They seemed to have passed over the east part of the city and were now going flat out for home.

As we neared the city I noticed that we were back down to twenty-one thousand feet, and our quarry seemed to be even a little lower, which meant they must be diving slightly. I recalled what other pilots had said about them: "After they drop their bombs they stick their noses down and go like a bat out of hell. If they've got a good start on you then, you haven't a hope of catching them." I didn't know whether or not these had dropped their bombs yet, but they obviously had their noses down, if they were losing altitude this fast, and they certainly seemed to be going some, too.

Suddenly a shower of little white objects like snowballs streaked past me from ahead, terrifying me because I thought they were some new kind of tracer bullets, and I looked around wildly for the enemy that was shooting at me. All I saw were the other Hurricanes though, and they seemed unperturbed. I couldn't imagine what was going on. It only lasted for a brief second. I wasn't to learn the explanation until after I landed.

We kept up the chase for a long way up in Malaya, following the bombers down and down, gradually gaining on them but not fast enough, for they finally made the safety of a cloudbank and we had to let them go. It was disappointing, but one gets used to disappointments in air warfare.

We didn't realize what the target of the raid had been until we were nearly back. Coming over our airdrome at three or four thousand feet, with the layer of low broken clouds making a sort of carpet just under us, I noticed through the spaces between the clouds a very light pall of thin blue smoke floating over the field. Then when I came through beneath the clouds the truth sank home as I saw that the airdrome was littered with dozens of fresh bomb craters!

Light blue and grey smoke was still wafting from the doors, windows, and eaves of the great hangars below. Near one hangar a Brewster Buffalo was burning furiously, wreathed in scarlet flames, with volumes of stormy black smoke rolling upward— obviously hit by an incendiary bomb.

So it appeared that our enemies, not content with shelling us out of all the airdromes on the north side of the island, were determined to drive us out completely by bombing this, our only base left.

Now we were faced with the ticklish problem of getting our Hurricanes down safely in the middle of all the bomb craters and debris, for there was of course no other field for us to land on. Reaching the drome a little ahead of the rest, I circled for several minutes, trying to figure out a way to land, "shooting" the field in fake approaches at low altitude from various directions— just as I had often done over pastures and Stubblefields back in America in barnstorming days— trying now to work out an imaginary runway between these craters.

Finally I made my choice, a short narrow stretch between the paths of several sticks of bombs, with water standing in the low area at one end and a cracked-up Hurricane which appeared to have just landed, lying on its belly near the other end. By this time I was leading a procession of all the rest of our Hurricanes around the field, all the pilots likewise trying to figure out how to get down. I made a try at my "runway," and made it all right, with room to spare, and then the rest followed in on it one after another, and everybody made it safely.

As soon as we'd reported to Operations on what happened, some of us went out with a truck and laid out some white boards to mark our landing strip.

While doing this we found a few enemy leaflets scattered about, and I realized that they must have been the little white things that streaked past me while we were up on the chase and gave me such a scare. I must have happened to fly through a cloud of them dropped by one of the bombers. I picked one up and kept it for a souvenir.

It was in English and purported to quote from a Lisbon news dispatch. Under the word "EXTRA" in large type it carried a heading, unpunctuated: "The Yankees Tender the Olive Branch Singapore Neutral Zone?" Then it read:

Lisbon, 14th: News has been received that America has proposed her separate peace negotiations to Nippon. The proposal was made on 14th January, 1942. President Roosevelt is of the opinion that Singapore ought to be declared a Neutral Zone. The Nippon is considering this peace proposal.

We arranged to have the cracked-up Hurricane moved out of our runway as soon as possible. It was the plane of Lieutenant S—, a South African Air Force pilot, better known as Stewie. I recalled the airplane that was missing from Denny's section shortly before we attacked the bombers. Apparently he was the one. He had got separated from us, found the bombers before we did and attacked them alone. He had shot one down in flames before he was himself wounded and shot down, force-landing on the drome, to be taken away to a hospital before the rest of us came back. The story of his unusual experiences on this and succeeding days is included later.

A crash truck arrived soon and took his machine out of the way, and the "runway" which we had marked off— a short narrow strip of sod in between rows of bomb craters — became our sole landing ground for the duration of our stay in Singapore.

Three of the boys from the other flight, who were on the ground, had a narrow escape during this raid. These were Joe, Fitz, and Tom, who had been loafing in the hotel after they went off duty when we relieved their flight. They heard us take off and heard the air-raid sirens a little later. Having nothing better to do they thought they'd take a drive to the airdrome to see what was going on. They took one of the cars, drove down East Coast Road, and were just turning in at the gate of the airdrome when the sentry there shouted to them and pointed upward.

Stopping the car, they climbed out just in time to actually see the bombs coming down in a great cluster. They only had time to throw themselves flat and cover their ears before the bombs were striking. Two big five-hundred-pounders landed, each about a hundred feet from them, one demolishing a house directly across the road!

Their car was holed in places by shrapnel, and one door was wrecked, while the boys themselves were bruised and blackened with dirt, their clothes torn, and they were badly shaken up. Fitz had to be taken to the hospital for treatment of shock, but was released the same day; Joe was told to stay off flying for a couple of days.

Poor Joe! It was he who had had two shells crash beside him at Tengah two days before. Then yesterday he'd been shot down and had crashed in the sea. So he was shelled one day, shot down the next, and bombed on the third!

It was nearly noon when we landed from this patrol. There were no other scrambles before one o'clock, when the other flight came back to relieve us. We doffed our mae wests, took our parachutes, helmets, and gloves out of our machines, put them away, and left the rest of the day's fighting to the other flight.

From the Communique:

Singapore, February 7. Enemy aircraft again raided the island this morning and bombs were dropped, causing some damage. Fighters of the Far East Command intercepted the raiders, destroying one enemy aircraft, probably destroying another, and damaging two. All our fighters returned to their bases.

At the Sea View the management were keeping a score-board of our successes, so when we came to lunch that noon we told them they could put down another enemy plane destroyed, as the result of Stewie's victory.

We were quite popular with most of the guests there those days, in spite of our rough everyday working dress which must have seemed out of place in such an exclusive hotel. Of course there were a few, the more blue-blooded, I suppose, who didn't take to us so well. Probably they thought the only legitimate officers were those they saw in peacetime at their exclusive dances, dressed in bandmasters' uniforms; so our usually boisterous return from work, in sweaty shorts and shirts (open-necked) with revolvers slung in rough service webbing, was quite beyond them.

One grumpy old codger in particular appeared to have nothing to do but sit around all day drinking pink gins and looking liverish and important. He was waiting for a boat to evacuate him, so that in addition to fighting to keep the Japs off his head now, we would quite likely have to patrol and perhaps fight over his ship later, to keep him from being sunk. His dislike for us was made obvious quite often. Some of the boys went for a dip in the hotel swimming pool on this afternoon, and he came snooping around and tried to chase them out, saying they couldn't swim there because they hadn't been "introduced"!

Among these boys was Brownie, and he rose nobly to the situation. "Well, my name's Browne. I guess that introduces me!" he replied. The others introduced themselves likewise and went on with their swimming.

The poor fellow retired quite perplexed, which, whether he knew it or not, was a good thing for him. The boys were trying to have enough fun to loose themselves from the strain they were under and would have thrown him in if he'd bothered them any more.

That night Rickey threw a little party to celebrate his promotion to squadron leader. He was able to get hold of some champagne, and a boisterous time was had by all. I've forgotten most of what went on, but remember that about halfway through the party someone remarked that he heard the Japs had landed on the island of Bali. We were all for taking off at once and going down there to make sure Dorothy Lamour escaped.

Next day was Sunday the eighth, and our flight had the "long day"— from dawn until 9:00 a.m. and from 1:00 p.m. until dark. It was quite uneventful for us, however. We had one routine patrol in the morning, and in the afternoon I did a convoy patrol with one other pilot, escorting a merchant ship out of the harbor and down the straits towards Sumatra for an hour or so. While we were doing this escort a big raid came over, which the rest of our flight chased unsuccessfully. I saw them drop their bombs in the north-east part of the island; that is, I saw the great mass of smoke clouds shooting up from the area as the bombs exploded, perhaps twenty miles away.

The other flight had a combat that morning, however, with an escorted bombing raid, in which they brought down at least two of the enemy. Rickey was shot down in this engagement and force-landed on the airdrome, his machine crashing through the fence on the north side and out onto East Coast Road, where it shed its landing gear in the ditch on one side, slid across the road on its belly, and stopped with its nose in the ditch on the other side. Rickey himself was unhurt— except for his feelings.

From the Communique:

Singapore, February 8. During enemy raids over Singapore Island this morning our fighters probably destroyed one enemy bomber. Two other bombers were damaged. All our fighters returned to their bases.

Chapter VII

Beginning of the End

On the whole, enemy air activity had been small for the past few days; but the next day, Monday, they really started crowding us.

Things began popping early. We had the short shift from 9:00 a.m. until 1:00 p.m. and I was awakened at dawn by the roar of engines as the other flight took off and climbed up over the hotel and off into the distance. They came back to land after an hour or so, while we were eating breakfast — not in one formation this time, but drifting in singly or in pairs, which meant they must have been in action.

They were off again in a short time, and when we reached the drome just before nine they were still flying, so that we had to wait a half hour or so for them.

Again they came back in scattered ones and twos, indicating they had been fighting. They looked pretty tired as they left their machines and came to the dispersal hut, but most of them were grinning triumphantly. There'd been numerous skirmishes and chases with low-flying bombers, and nearly every pilot had had one or more shots.

Sandy A—, a very aggressive pilot of 175, had got two bombers, bringing his total score to five. Sergeant H—, one of my group from 300 Squadron, had got one also, his first victory. He said he dived on a bomber which he found alone up in Malaya, and fired on it. As he pulled away he looked around furtively to see if it was shooting back at him, and was quite amazed to see it go into a spin instead. He watched it crash in the jungle! Three or four other bombers were damaged too, while our boys suffered no losses.

I took over Sandy's machine, and he warned me that it had a "runaway" gun— a machine-gun that worked all right except that it wouldn't stop firing once it started, until it used up all its ammunition. The armorers were working on it and would get it fixed up if they had time. Others of our flight took over the rest of the machines, and the boys who had been flying made off to the hotel for breakfast.

Hardly had we settled down to waiting, when the telephone rang, and the message was "Scramble to twenty thousand feet at once!"

It would be the regular morning high-altitude raid approaching, and the eight of us raced to our machines. I was halfway into my cockpit before I realized something was wrong: armorers were still sitting on the wings of my airplane, working, with the big panels still off above the guns.

The armorer sergeant was looking distressed. "I'm sorry, sir, we haven't had time to reload your guns yet. Yours is the last machine we came to. We'll get them done as quick as we can."

There was no one to blame. The crews were overworked and this scramble had come too soon after the planes landed to give them time to finish. I climbed in and got set, waiting impatiently, while other machines started and taxied out. The armorers were working feverishly on my guns, snatching out empty ammunition tanks and fastening new ones in, threading fresh belts through the chutes that led into the guns. Roar after roar of sound swept across the field as the four planes of Denny's section took off, one after another in quick order. Then my own section was taking off, leaderless. I hoped Brownie would know enough to take over the lead. Of all the lousy luck!

At last the armorers were putting the panels back over the openings in the wings above the guns, and I primed my engine and pressed the starter button. The engine caught and started idling. The seven other Hurricanes were far out over the harbor now, one section of four and the other section— mine— only three, all climbing fast.

Finally the last panel was in place, the men were sliding down off the wings, and the sergeant waved the "go ahead" signal with his hands. I taxied out as fast as I dared, but by the time I was off, the others were entirely out of sight. There was nothing to do now but to go "free lance," for there was slight chance of finding the others once I'd lost sight of them.

I abused my engine terribly climbing nearly wide open, for now that I was alone I was extra anxious to have a height advantage before the enemy got over the island.

My lot was frustration again, however, for in spite of all my furious climbing I was scarcely fifteen thousand feet up when I saw enemy planes coming in over the island. Hoping they might hang around a few minutes I kept climbing anyway, careful to stay four or five miles away from under them so I wouldn't be spotted while below them and jumped by their escorting fighters. But within a couple of minutes after I saw them they had turned away and were making northward at high speed. Out of luck again!

After that, Control kept reporting smaller formations at various altitudes, which seemed to nip in over the north part of the island for a few minutes and then go away before there was time to find them; or sometimes to do standing patrols a little way up in enemy territory.

I spent an hour or so free-lancing around, mostly at high altitude, hoping to find one of these groups when I was in a position to jump them. Two or three times I spotted a couple of fighters in the distance and carefully stalked them until I got above and upsun. Then I went down in screaming dives to attack, only to find when I got close enough to identify them that they were Hurricanes— others of our flight, doing the same thing I was. It looked as if they must have got split up somehow, and I wondered if they'd had a scrap.

The scenery at high altitude was magnificent that morning. Gigantic tumbled masses of cloud rose to fifteen and twenty thousand feet, beautiful and awe-inspiring with their great misty mountains, valleys and chasms, with here and there a detached cloud like an island suspended by magic in the sky. It was all so enchanting that once or twice when I was waiting for information from Control I surrendered to temptation, and swooped down among them to play about for a couple of minutes, diving at their tops, careening at four hundred miles an hour through great foggy valleys and in and out of weird mystic caverns half a mile deep, occasionally shearing away to practise a few rolls.

Far off below, a level carpet of broken fluffy clouds lay over the island, obscuring most of the countryside. Through it ran the mantle of oil-fire smoke, a long belt in which the black and white clouds churned and writhed together, endlessly, like two flavors of boiling hot blanc-mange, chocolate and steamy white, slowly mixing.

Somewhere under the south part of that carpet would be our hotel — no bigger than a pinhead — and the old grouch who tried to chase the boys out of the swimming pool, still sitting on the veranda, no doubt, with his pink gins and his liver and his dislike for the world. What a narrow life he led. Perhaps most of ours were short, but they were wide as we could make them while they lasted, anyway!

At last I got wind of something worth-while. I had been sitting at around twenty thousand, when Control reported "fifteen plus bandits" just north of the island at fourteen thousand feet. This was just what I wanted, something below my altitude, and I swooped off in that direction, hoping to catch them silhouetted against the clouds below. However, I must have arrived too late, for I couldn't find anything in the area. I was getting worried that they might find me first, when I happened to spot far below, through an opening in the low clouds, the shapes of two twin-engined bombers, crossing the straits at very low level, going northward toward home!

They were almost directly beneath me, so I peeled off in a nearly vertical dive. I had to lose sight of them on the way down, for it was only a small opening in the clouds through which I'd seen them, but I gauged my dive to break through the clouds where I thought they should be.

I was in an awful sweat, for I was in high hopes that my luck had changed at last. This was the closest I'd come to getting a shot yet. I imagine I was doing nearly five hundred when I passed through the clouds, for I had to just fly in a long great circle for a few seconds after I levelled out, to get my speed down to where I could maneuver. I was looking vainly all around for the bombers, but though I searched frantically for several minutes I failed to spot them. Either I had misjudged the course they were taking or they had climbed up into the clouds for concealment. I was several miles up in enemy territory when I finally gave up the search.

On the way back I spotted a truck parked on the road and put a burst into it from my guns. As I fired I was fascinated to see what looked like long weird ropes of white smoke suddenly streak far out ahead from my wings, snakily, their farther ends touching the truck or near it. It was the first time I had ever fired "tracer" ammunition. The special bullets are coated with chemicals to give off smoke, to show you where your bullets are going. The squadrons I'd served with in England never used it, but 175 Squadron did. The only times I'd seen tracers before were when German pilots shot at me, for all German squadrons use them.

When I stopped firing at the truck and turned away I was again startled by the runaway gun which Sandy had warned me about. Now it rattled away on its own, firing at nothing, until it was out of ammunition!

About this time, Control ordered us to return and land unless we were engaged, so I headed homeward.

We'd hardly had time to get refueled and rearmed after this flight when we were ordered to scramble again. Another big high altitude raid was on the way, and we took off in a rush, climbing madly even before we had joined up in formation. Then after a couple of minutes a new order came over the radio from Control.

"Hello, Tiger Leader, Tiger Leader! There are low-lying aircraft attacking our troops in the northwest part of the island. Detach two of your aircraft to deal with them. Over!"

Denny's voice came across at once, acknowledging the order, and then he called to me: "Hello, Blue One, Blue One! Will you take your number two and take care of that? Over."

"O.K.," I answered. "Hello, Blue Two. Follow me!" And I led off in a diving turn into the northwest, leaving the others to climb on up after the big raid. My number two's name was Sergeant M—.

Control called again, urging us to hurry, and we opened our engines to full throttle as we swept down under the clouds towards the area given. As we neared it I strained my eyes trying to discern any airplanes there, or anti-aircraft puffs which would indicate their presence, but I could see neither. We arrived and circled that part of the island low down, watching in all directions without seeing anything. Finally I called Control.

"Hello, Rastus. Hello, Rastus! Tiger Blue One calling. We are in the area but we don't see anything about. I'm afraid we're too late. Have you any new instructions for us?"

But I never gave him time to reply, for a couple of seconds later I saw it. We were traveling north just then, toward the section of the straits where the Johore Causeway crossed into the enemy-occupied city of Johore Bharu, and I caught sight of an airplane in the distance straight ahead, low down over Johore Bharu and traveling north.

I fumbled excitedly for the transmitter switch. "Tally-ho! Straight ahead of us, Blue Two!" I called, and laid out after it, pushing throttle and propeller pitch controls clear ahead, and this time "pulling the plug" also— a control which cuts out all governing over the engine's supercharging so that it can put out an emergency power far greater than its normal maximum.

The sound rose to an immense, strained bellowing, and in a few seconds my controls began to stiffen from the increased speed, and the countryside seemed to fairly stream past, close beneath our wings, for we were flying low down over the trees.

Crossing the Straits of Johore we streaked low across the rooftops of Johore Bharu, chasing our quarry, who was now following along the main highway which leads northwest from the city up into Malaya. I remember noticing that the road was packed with military traffic — enemy trucks, busses, cars, etc.

The enemy plane had a good start on us, and at first we hardly seemed to gain on it. We started getting flak (anti-aircraft fire) — the first Japanese flak I'd seen. There was just an occasional black puff near us at first; then soon a regular hail of it, following us right along. It seemed to make about the same sized bursts as the British and German "medium" flak — Bofors and Pom-pom guns — with the differences that this stuff seemed to have adjustable fuses so that it was timed to explode near us, and that it had no tracer effect, remaining invisible until it exploded. Ours and the German medium flak doesn't explode unless it actually hits you or reaches the end of its travel, and the shells are all tracers, appearing as red or green balls. We were so intent on overtaking our quarry that we just let them blaze away, without taking any evasive action from the shells.

At last we were gaining noticeably on the other machine, and soon I could discern its shape as that of a single-engined plane with "fixed" (non-retractable) landing gear hanging down. From pictures I'd seen I took it to be a type of two-seat fighter known as the "Army 97." It alternately flew at about five hundred feet for a minute or so and then dived to treetop height for a way, where we could scarcely see it against the jungle. We stayed at about five hundred feet ourselves. Behind me a couple of hundred yards Sergeant M—'s plane, guarding my tail, appeared as a vicious silhouette against a background of angry anti-aircraft puffs sprinkled pepper-like against the sky.

I think I was perhaps four or five hundred yards behind our quarry, for I remember that I already had my thumb on the firing button ready to press it in a few more seconds, when the beginning occurred, of one of those nightmare experiences that last actually but a moment but live forever after in inescapable memory.

First a bright flash of color caught my eye. I was staring down fascinated at a green Navy Zero wheeling across below and ahead of me, turning steep left just above the treetops, while seemingly without any conscious decision I was twisting over viciously in a diving turn after him. I closed in, still diving, pulling my nose around until my sights lined up with him and a little ahead, leading him, then letting him have it, the quick, shattering roar from my guns startling me, and my long white tracers reaching out to caress the graceful little green wings ahead of me with their strange red discs painted near each tip. Only for two or three seconds, and then I had to break off to straighten out of my dive before hitting the trees. Just as I was breaking off I heard a bang and felt a jolt, and saw that one of the smaller gun panels was gone from my right wing. I thought it had been shot off; but I forgot about it in what I saw a moment later.

I zoomed up hard, nearly blacking out and just missing the trees. My runaway gun was chattering away on its own irritatingly and spewing its tracers aimlessly out over the jungle. I turned left to get around at any new enemies that might be behind. And there, amid the confusion of anti-aircraft fire bursting all around, I saw Sergeant M—'s Hurricane diving steeply, obviously hit! I was right over him as he struck, in the corner of a little field, at close to three hundred miles an hour, in a terrible ghastly eruption of splintered wings and flying pieces and then steam and dust and smoke that swirled out to obscure the awful sight.

I recall circling cautiously for a moment, dazed and shocked by this and trying to take in the whole situation and see how many new enemies I had. In doing so I apparently lost sight of both the one we'd been chasing and the Navy Zero. There were no new ones to be seen either.

Thinking back on the event, I believe the Navy Zero pilot must have been above us when he saw us chasing the other Jap, so he dived on us from behind, firing and hitting Sergeant M—. Then his speed carried him on down and ahead as he leveled out from his dive, until he was below and in front of me where I first saw him. Sergeant M— must either have been killed by the bullets or had his controls disabled, and went into the fatal dive that I saw.

A pathetic little wisp of smoke and dust rising above the trees was the last I saw of him, as escorted by the storm of anti-aircraft fire I made my way alone back to Singapore Island.

Control was telling the others about another raid coming in at high altitude, so I headed out over the sea and started climbing. I was late again though, for I saw the bombers approaching the island when I was far too low. In fact I was able to call up Control and correct him on the position he was giving for them once or twice, while still unable to do anything myself except look up at them and swear. When they were almost over the island they turned away and headed out seaward. Later I learned that some of the others chased them and got in a few good shots, damaging two or three.

After they had gone away I did a little free-lancing again but nothing more turned up, and finally Control ordered all of us to land. I was down before the rest, and when the others landed and came up to the dispersal hut I had to give

them the news of Sergeant M—'s death. I hadn't known him well, but the mute faces and glistening eyes of some of the boys told me how much they thought of him. I wondered if any of them felt it was my fault.

Late that afternoon, Denny, Ted, Brownie, and I drove into town to take care of some business, after which we stopped in at the Raffles Hotel for a drink. Ted had a brother who was a captain in the Singapore police force, and while we were there he dropped in and joined us. — It was from him that we heard the incredible news.

The enemy had forced the Straits of Johore during the preceding night and landed "in force" on the north part of the island!

There was supposed to be heavy fighting going on in the jungles and rubber estates around Tengah Airdrome now. No one seemed to know what it meant or how serious the situation, but it sounded ominous. That explained the sudden spurt in enemy air activity this morning!

I realized that the orange crush I was drinking didn't taste good any more. The siege was over and the enemy inside our gates. Was the thing we couldn't let happen, really occurring? Was Singapore falling? I didn't know much about military strategy, but it seemed to me that if we couldn't hold them at the straits we had slight chance of holding them anywhere on the island.

Apparently this news had been broadcast at noon, but we hadn't listened to the news. It failed to interrupt the evening dance program at the Raffles, however; for before we left, the orchestra men were collecting on the platform.

Back at the Sea View that evening we learned from the boys of the other flight that the afternoon had been a field day for them. The island had been teeming with small groups of bombers and dive-bombers, mostly unescorted, at low altitude. Everyone in the flight had got at least one crack at them, and they had destroyed five or six as well as getting a bunch of probables. Sandy, the boy who had got two in the morning, got another in the afternoon to make his score three for the day, six for his total score to date. They lost two machines, but the pilot of one got away unhurt and the other escaped alive although badly wounded.

By now we could hear distant artillery fire most of the time. That night it was louder than ever, with the explosions of shells sounding closer.

From the Communique:

Singapore, February 9. An enemy force in strength succeeded in landing on the western shores of Singapore Island last night. They are being engaged by our troops. Fighting continues.

Hurricane fighters of the R.A.F. supporting our troops successfully intercepted enemy raiders today, destroying three, probably destroying three others and damaging thirteen.

In a later patrol our fighter aircraft wrecked an enemy truck during a road strafe.

By now we were all looking forward to the next day in anticipation of good hunting. No doubt there'd be lots of bombers operating in close support of enemy troops, flying at low altitude where we could get at them easily.

Our hopes were all dashed, however, by a new order that came through for the squadron that night; they were to take off all their flyable Hurricanes at dawn and evacuate them to Palembang, in Sumatra (where 300 Squadron were)! It had been decided not to risk losing all our Hurricanes at once, as we would, should this, our only remaining airdrome, get bombed any worse or come under shell-fire from the advancing enemy. Also there was a pressing need for more airplanes at Palembang.

This last gave credence to a disquieting rumor we heard from someone that night— that Palembang had been heavily raided during the past two or three days and that 300 Squadron (my squadron), who were defending the place, had been badly "beaten up" by overwhelming numbers.

There were eight machines to go, and the pilots who flew them were all taken from regular 175 Squadron pilots, so we five attached pilots from 300 Squadron were among those staying behind. Those who went were met in the dispersal hut next morning by the "A.O.C.," the officer commanding all the air forces in the area. He talked to them a few minutes before they left.

He told them he understood their keenness and desire to stay on in Singapore, but he gave them a picture of the situation. He said that during the day before, more than two hundred and fifty enemy airplanes had been over the island; that we had hunted and fought them all day, only eight strong ourselves, but that we couldn't expect to keep up such a pace. So he was sending the airplanes to Palembang, where they were just as badly needed now as here, and where the operating conditions were much more favorable.

We others didn't mind being left behind. There were rumors that a fresh squadron might come up in a day or so, if the military situation got stabilized. If there was any chance to do some fighting we wanted to be in it. Singapore just couldn't be allowed to go under!

About midmorning we five from 300 Squadron drove out to Operations—which were in a large house commandeered by the R.A.F. a couple of miles from the hotel— to see what we could learn.

The Operations Room had apparently been the living room of the house. A sort of stage about three feet high was erected at one end, where the controller and operations staff sat behind a counter which contained at least a dozen telephones and microphones, and bristled with switches and connections.

It overlooked the "operations board," a huge map several feet across, of Singapore Island, Southern Malaya, and the surrounding sea and islands. Positions of all "plots" of our own or enemy planes were marked by little blocks of wood on this board, moved about by assistants wearing telephone head-sets, on the basis of information they received on their phones. This was how the information on enemy aircraft was put into picture form for the controllers. It was from here that our air operations were directed — the controller speaking to us in the air with one of the microphones and ordering us about on the basis of the situation as he saw it pictured on this board.

The controller on duty this morning was Squadron Leader C—, whom Denny knew quite well. He had been C.O. of 300 Squadron back in England during the preceding spring and summer. We found him at his post in the Operations Room, though there was nothing for him to do — there weren't any airplanes for him to control now.

He was seated at the counter, idly watching the plots of enemy aircraft on the board below him, as the assistants moved the blocks of wood about. We saw one marked "Thirty plus, 22,000 feet" a couple of feet north of the edge of Singapore Island on the map; an arrow, showing its direction, pointed south. There were three or four other blocks representing smaller formations scattered about.

He could tell us little, except to advise us to hang on and wait for orders. He'd heard little of how the fighting was going this morning. Someone remarked that he'd heard Tengah Airdrome had been captured. "Is it?" the Squadron Leader asked. "Let's call them up and see!" With a little grin he picked up one of his telephones, which was a direct line to Tengah. The line was ominously silent.

We drove back to the hotel and loafed about. After a while a nurse came around, looking for someone with a car who would help evacuate some other nurses from a hospital a few miles away which had come under shell-fire. Denny became chivalrous and volunteered. He drove off, looking a little sheepish and answering with some defensive retort our rude remarks about his motives.

He came back inside of an hour with six nurses in the car, all in varying stages of fright. The air-raid sirens sounded just then and they all made for the shelter trenches among the palm trees out on the lawn. We pilots sat on the grass around the trenches and chatted with them while a formation of bombers droned across far above, escorted by the white puffs of heavy anti-aircraft shells around them.

Soon the all clear sounded and the nurses climbed out of the trenches. One of them, a frail-appearing little lady, seemed to be having quite a time to control herself. She was trembling all over and weaved a little when she started to walk.

"Somebody ki-ick me under the chi-in!" she asked in a quavering but resolute little voice, and we all laughed. She was wearing a soldier's steel helmet, which alone was enough to make us laugh, it looked so funny in contrast with her meek dress and mouse-like demeanor.

We invited them into the lounge adjacent to my room, and Denny produced a bottle of Johnnie Walker that he'd rescued from the ruins of the Officers' Mess at Kallang. We had a boy get some glasses and gave them each a drink or two. It did them a lot of good and they soon relaxed and forgot most of their fright.

The frail little lady who had asked to be kicked under the chin told us that she'd spent her honeymoon in this hotel years before. She said she was a planter's wife and had lived near Kluang, a town fifty or sixty miles up in Malaya. That was the first I'd heard of Kluang except as the location of the nearest enemy-occupied airdrome to Singapore.

Finally they took their leave, Denny driving them to the hospital to which their patients had been moved.

The day was bright and sunny now, the sky clear except where the mantle of oil-fire smoke stretched across, augmented now by that from a second fire which seemed to be burning near the original one. Enemy planes were operating over the north part of the island in large numbers, but seldom came over far enough south for us to see them. It was fairly peaceful yet except for the distant rumbling of artillery. We could see several large ships riding quietly at anchor in the harbor as if nothing was wrong. We thought it a miracle that they hadn't yet been bombed.

The enemy might be approaching and the number of guests rapidly decreasing, but the hotel routine went on as usual. At four in the afternoon the same friendly little Chinese boy brought tea and cakes to my room, grinning happily and jabbering unintelligibly and good-naturedly the while. Supper in the evening consisted of seven courses as usual, delicious and expertly cooked, complete with French names on the menu that always made the dishes a surprise for us when they were brought on.

The guests who still remained were dismayed when they learned that our Hurricanes had left. It must have seemed a very bad omen to them. We told them we hoped a new squadron would arrive shortly. They commented to us, as others had, that one of the biggest helps to the morale of the people during the last few days of frightening news and frequent air raids had been the sight of our little band of Hurricanes taking off and climbing up over the city time after time each day to engage the enemy. No matter how bad the news, as long as they could see the R.A.F. still flying they felt there was hope.

From the Communique:

Singapore, February 10. The enemy has maintained continuous dive-bombing and machine-gun attacks on our forward areas in the western sector throughout the day, as well as high-level bombing attacks by large formations of aircraft.

London, February 10 (AP). The Vichy radio broadcast today a Japanese communique saying that all British airdromes on Singapore Island had been captured.

That night the artillery fire was definitely much closer, so we knew the battle was going badly. A sullen red glow lit up a large part of the sky north of us. One battery of two heavy guns had started operating near enough to shake the hotel each time they fired. All night long the more distant rumbling was interrupted every few minutes by the vehement booming of this pair, like two doors being slammed in another part of the building.

As always in Singapore, I slept with my revolver under my pillow, and this time I kept my doors locked, too. But my only intruder was the grinning Chinese boy who brought in my cup of tea early next morning.

Two of the boys had been detailed the night before to get up early and be driven to Seletar Airdrome on the north-east side of the island, to bring back a couple of damaged Hurricanes which had been fixed up so they would fly. They turned up again before breakfast, having done their job, and told of a creepy trip going over there in the darkness, being stopped and examined frequently at the point of bayonets along the blacked-out road, scared each time that they'd run into an enemy trap, until they could see who had stopped them. They said the airdrome had been captured the afternoon before, but our troops had retaken it in the evening. They were preparing to blow up the field as soon as the boys had taken off.

And still it was cool, quiet, and peaceful where we sat on the veranda of the hotel, that morning, only a few miles from the fighting— less, for all we knew. The artillery fire had quieted down with the coming of daylight. Denny and I were enthralled for a while watching an exotic, dark-haired English girl clad in shorts and a light sweater, exercising with two greyhounds among the palm trees out on the lawn. She was swinging a cloth about for them to leap at. Her movements and theirs were so graceful that I thought she must be a dancer, but someone said she was a nurse. It seemed that either she or the approaching enemy and the terrible fighting must be unreal. It just didn't make sense — but neither did a lot of things, in the last days of Singapore.

The Singapore morning papers came at breakfast time just as usual, though we could now see a fire started by shell-fire in the north part of town. We read them just as usual over our lavish breakfasts. I still have the copy I bought that morning, the February nth issue of the Singapore Free Press. Printed and gotten out full-size while the enemy were almost inside the city, it gives all the local and world news. Its front-page editorial calls on its readers to be "determined and defiant."

Chapter VIII

Evacuation

After breakfast, Denny, Ted, Brownie, and I drove to the airdrome to see what we could find out, but no one seemed to know anything. We'd hoped there'd be news of the fresh Hurricane squadron which we had heard was coming, but

Tom W—, who was doing duty pilot (looking after the phones, etc.), said he hadn't heard anything.

A couple of new fires were pumping black smoke into the sky north of us, and the familiar high smoke pall looked much heavier than before, frightening. It was drifting right across the city, most of which was darkened by its shadow. Was that an omen?

I climbed up on the side of a dispersal pen and snapped three views with my camera, one west, one northwest, and one north. Only the first one, showing the harbor and south part of the city, is innocent of smoke.

An air-raid warning was on but we weren't paying attention, until we heard the familiar heavy droning from above; then we all made for some trenches. When we reached their safety we looked up and spotted the bombers, a standard formation of twenty-seven, slowly drilling across the sky above us but passing a little to one side, so we knew our airdrome couldn't be the target. They were passing over the harbor and south part of the town, a couple of miles away.

All at once someone called out and pointed towards the city. In the harbor near the docks several great columns of water were rising majestically to a height of perhaps two hundred feet. Then dozens of smoke clouds shot up in a row across the dock area, swirling stormily together while the awful staccato booming of the explosions reached us, shaking the ground under our feet.

I got out my camera and took another snap of this area, to contrast with the one I'd taken a few minutes before when there were no smoke clouds.

We hoped that none of the ships in the harbor were hit. I learned later that they weren't, but a lot of damage must have been done to the docks and near-by buildings. A couple of good-sized fires got going there within a few minutes, putting up a lot of black smoke.

Finally satisfied that there was nothing we could find out here we piled into the car and drove out to Operations, to see what we could learn. We found our friend. Squadron Leader C—, on duty again when we arrived, sitting at his post overlooking the operations board which showed nothing but plots of Japanese formations, just as we had found him the day before.

He was speaking to someone over the telephone, and we caught the words as we came in: "—I refuse to have anything more to do with air-raid warnings. You might just as well keep the warning on permanently!"

He bid us good morning as he replaced the receiver, then pointed his thumb at the phone and snorted, "A.R.P., just onto me about air-raid warnings! With more Jap formations around than you can shake a stick at. I can't tell them when one's going to nip in and take a crack at the city!"

We laughed sympathetically.

"Got any news for us yet?" Denny asked.

"No, I haven't heard anything," the squadron leader answered. "Tell you what," he reached for another phone, "I'll talk to Air Headquarters and see if I can find out anything."

He asked the operator at Air Headquarters for a certain official, and a discussion followed for two or three minutes. Midway through the conversation he turned and spoke to Denny. "Do you know how many Hurricanes there are at Kallang Airdrome that can be flown?"

"Three," Denny replied. He was counting the two which had been flown over from Seletar Airdrome early this morning, and one other which had been fixed up at Kallang.

The squadron leader passed this information on over the phone. At the end of the conversation he turned to Denny with the verdict: "You're to take the two other most experienced pilots with you and fly the three Hurricanes down to Palembang!"

So that was that. Our part in the battle for Singapore was over!

Brownie and I were the other two to go with Denny, and when we drove back to the hotel we parked the car close to our rooms and began loading our bags into it. I still had Bruce's bag which I was keeping to send to his folks, and I loaded it in with my things. We weren't hurrying, as we might have if we had known what we were going to learn shortly; it was perhaps an hour from the time we left Operations before we reached the airdrome accompanied by Ted, who was seeing us off.

As we drove up to the dispersal hut Tom, the boy who was doing duty pilot, came running out to meet us. He had his overalls and mae west on, and looked very excited.

"Where've you fellows been all this time?" he demanded. Then, not waiting for an answer, "We've got to hurry. The Japs are almost here! I'm going with you; they've got a Brewster fixed up so it will fly and I'm taking it— if I can figure out how it works. Squadron Leader C—'s called up three times in the last twenty minutes, asking if you've got here yet. He kept saying, 'Tell them they must hurry! Tell them they haven't a minute to waste!' He was awfully excited."

We rummaged hastily around in the hut, looking for maps of our route.

"So that's how it is," Denny remarked. "I reckon things must be getting bad fast at that rate!"

"It sounds as if Squadron Leader C—'s seen the Japs," I suggested. "They could come right past Operations without noticing it was any different from another private house."

We had trouble finding maps of Sumatra. Denny finally got a pretty good one, which he would use because he was leading us, and I got part of an old naval chart that showed the coastline of Sumatra and the River Musi which ran from the coast inland to Palembang. I stuck it in my pocket for emergency.

All three Hurricanes we were taking were in questionable condition, having been patched up and put together hurriedly, but the hard working New Zealand ground crews were doing all they could for them. Whatever we accomplished in those last few days of operating at Kallang, we owed largely to these ground crews — who worked night and day and through bombing and machine-gun attacks, never losing spirit and always keeping our machines in shape if it was humanly possible. The ground crews at Kallang Airdrome were a real fighting bunch, as grand as those who earned an undying reputation at Hawkinge and Manston, the R.A.F.'s front-line refueling and rearming bases during the Battle of Britain.

Each of us picked a machine, and began carrying our bags to it. Mine was in a dispersal pen about fifty yards away; to save distance I climbed over the back of the pen, taking my parachute, helmet, and gloves on the first trip. Tossing them into the cockpit I hurried back for another load. Ted was helping us get our things unloaded from the car. He and the rest of the fellows were going to try to find a ship on which they could travel to Palembang.

All at once we heard a sharp explosion from a grove just northeast of us, and then an answering explosion overhead. Looking up we saw a round black cloud, a couple of hundred feet high, over the middle of the airdrome. "Oh, oh!" I thought. "So they are almost here!"

I lugged three bags over to my Hurricane. Where to put all my things was a problem, for I couldn't possibly take time to hunt for ropes and tie them in, and if they were loose in the wrong places they'd foul the controls. Perhaps we shouldn't be taking time to put in our bags at all.

The gun in the grove fired again, and another shell burst over the drome.

I had borrowed a screwdriver, and working feverishly I loosened the panels in the side of the fuselage of my machine and took them off. I managed to get a small bag on the floor under the control cables. There was a large removable tray in one place, containing emergency rations, water, and first-aid equipment for use in the event of a forced landing in the jungle. I loosened this, jerked it out, and tried to stuff into its place a parachute bag full of clothes and things. But there was no bottom to the cavity left by the tray, and I saw despairingly that the bag wanted to sink down and rest on the control cables just below.

Another explosion came from the gun in the grove. This time the shell burst right above us. I ducked under the tail for a moment to escape any shrapnel bits. Wondering how many more minutes we had, I hastily unstrapped the tins and boxes of supplies and water from the tray I had taken out, then put the tray back in place, empty. By dint of a lot of shoving and squeezing I got a second bag in on top of the tray, quite secure. Two of them taken care of. For the rest I'd have to take the big panel off the bottom of the fuselage and jam them in on the bottom framework, under the elevator and rudder cables, hoping the cables wouldn't rub too hard or catch on them.

I looked for my screwdriver to take off this panel, but it was gone, and I started going in circles before remembering that Brownie had borrowed it for a moment.

And then I heard the sound that froze me inside — the unmistakable cracks of rifle-fire, and close — not more than a quarter of a mile away!

Denny was putting his things into his machine twenty or thirty yards away, and we exchanged sickly grins.

"I reckon we better hurry," he remarked, which I thought should take a prize for understatement. I'd have to make the rest of this darn quick!

I sprinted back after the last two bags, which were still in the car, and then— horror of horrors— the car was gone!

Now I was running in circles! There wasn't a sign of either the car or Ted. Had he got scared and pulled out? I was agonized, for one of the bags was Bruce's. I hated to leave mine and couldn't leave his.

I ran over to Brownie's machine to get my screwdriver. He said Ted had driven over to the hangar for something and would probably be back in a minute. I'd just have to wait. I had locked those two bags in the trunk of the car; all the rest had been piled in the back seat. Ted obviously didn't know about those in the trunk.

Down the field a little way we could hear the whine of an American inertia starter speeding up — Tom was trying to get the Brewster started. I took the screwdriver back to my machine, replaced the side panels, then took off the bottom one, and stuffed my third bag in the bottom of the fuselage.

Over the city a couple of enemy reconnaissance planes were cruising peacefully, at low altitude.

It was torture to wait. I climbed up beside the cockpit and began to turn the gas on and fix everything else so I could start up quickly. Denny, finished with his packing, stood by his airplane watching me, trying to conceal his anxiety.

"You almost ready?" he asked, with a good attempt at a matter-of-fact tone. To Denny, the worst sin he could commit would be to ever "flap" or appear excited.

"I can't go yet, Denny," I told him. "Ted's driven over to the hangar with the car and it's got Bruce's bag in it. I've got to wait!"

The cracking of rifles was growing in volume, and seemed to be getting a little closer. Occasionally a bullet or two whined close overhead. The fence and shrubbery on the edge of the airdrome made it impossible for us to see what was happening on the other side.

A little biplane with British markings came cruising over at three or four hundred feet, and I recognized it as a training machine that had been left at Tengah Airdrome. Some Jap pilot must be taking a ride in it!

The enemy gun in the woods, which had been putting shells over the airdrome, sent two or three after the little plane, the gunners assuming that it was one of our pilots, I suppose. I thought it would have been a good joke on them if they'd hit it.

Over the city the two reco machines still cruised around lazily.

Bizarre? I'll say it was! Everything I can remember about that morning is bizarre!

Finally Denny called, "Here's your car!"

Ted was just driving up in front of the dispersal hut. I raced over frantically, unlocked the trunk with the duplicate set of keys I had in my pocket, and jerked the precious bags out. Then I tore back to my machine and started stuffing them in the bottom of the fuselage.

Tom had his Brewster started now, and was taxiing out to the end of the "runway." A couple of ground crew chaps, who had arrived to help, told me to get in while they put the panel back under the fuselage for me. Good fellows. They were sticking with us to the last, Japs or no Japs.

I clambered up into the cockpit, and when I got my straps and helmet fastened, turned to look at Denny, who was in his cockpit waiting. He leaned ahead to press his starter button, and his engine came to life. I carefully measured two strokes from my priming pump, pressed my own starter button, and felt a thrill of relief as my engine caught instantly. "Anyway, it starts," I thought.

We taxied out, picking our way carefully among the bomb craters and soft spots until we reached the end of the runway, where Tom already waited for us in his idling Brewster. Brownie followed in his Hurricane. Pausing to let Denny start off first, I looked back furtively, half expecting to see Jap soldiers entering the drome and getting ready to pot at us; but all I saw were Ted and two or three other pilots and some ground crew chaps in a little knot around the car, probably discussing what to do. As Denny's machine rocketed down the runway I turned and opened my throttle, following him.

We made one circuit of the airdrome after we took off, and were followed by Japanese anti-aircraft fire — the first time I was ever shot at by enemy anti-aircraft fire over my own drome!

I had my camera in my pocket, and while we were making this circuit I took a snap of the north part of the city, where a huge ugly fire was raging among a lot of buildings. We turned and headed southward out over the sea. When we were out two or three miles I took another snap over the tail of my machine — presumably the last air picture of Singapore, outside of any taken by the enemy.

My final memory of Singapore, as it appeared to me looking back for the last time, is of a bright green little country, resting on the edge of the bluest sea I'd ever seen, lovely in the morning sunlight except where the dark tragic mantle of smoke ran across its middle and beyond, covering and darkening the city on the seashore.

The city itself, with huge leaping red fires in its north and south parts, appeared to rest on the floor of a vast cavern formed by the sinister curtains of black smoke which rose from beyond and towered over it, prophetically, like a great overhanging cloak of doom.

Chapter IX

Stewie's Escape

I think this would be a good place to tell the story of Stewie (Lieutenant S—), the South African boy of 175 Squadron who was shot down on the day Kallang Airdrome was bombed, as described in Chapter VI. This is almost word for word as he told it to me nearly a month later, on a hospital ship in the Indian Ocean. After writing it down I read it back to him, and he O.K.'d it:

"You remember when we were scrambled that morning and climbed up after the big raid that was coming in at twenty thousand feet or above? Well, I was leading a pair on the right of the formation, in Denny's section, and when we started getting up around twenty thousand feet I noticed my engine wasn't running right and I couldn't keep up with the rest of you. So I signaled my number two to leave me behind and go on with you, and I kept falling back until you were two or three miles ahead of me. All at once I looked off to the left and saw this mass of bombers coming in from the southwest.

"They were a little lower than I was, and I called out 'Tally-Ho!' and went after them. I guess you were so far away by that time that you were never able to get close enough to attack, but I was just right. I came in behind them, making for the nearest and coming in at him from the left and behind. The whole bunch started shooting at me and there were dozens of tracers coming from all directions, mostly seeming to converge just in front of me. Boy, it was just as though they were laying a smoke screen! I held my fire though, until I was right up close to this fellow: then I let him have it from almost point-blank range.

"His rear gunner packed up and quit firing right away. Then smoke started coming back from the fuselage, and I turned so my fire was going into his left engine, which began smoking right away. I thought, 'Well, this guy's had it!' So I turned to attack another and just then 'WHAM' I got it! The explosion threw me sideways in the seat and just seemed to stop my plane in midair. Then my cockpit was full of oil and steam and glycol and stuff so I couldn't see, and I thought this was no place for me; so I peeled off and dived for good old Mother Earth!

"I knew my leg was hit, because there was blood all over it, but it didn't hurt and I felt all right. However, I was still in an awful pickle when I tried to land, because there was so much oil and glycol and stuff all over my windshield that I couldn't see ahead. I decided to try to make it 'wheels up.'

"I could see the field when I was circling it, by looking out the side of my cockpit, but when I was making my approach to land, coming straight towards it, I couldn't see the field at all because of the stuff all over my windshield. I could tell by the buildings and high trees on each side where it should be, and I just steered in between them and hoped. I came in real fast, trusting to luck that I'd miss the bomb craters, touched down at well over a hundred miles an hour and slid to a nice stop in the middle of the field.

"I got out and looked at my airplane. By luck I'd landed in the one place on the whole field that wasn't full of fresh bomb craters. I sat down in front of my machine, and after a couple of minutes a car drove up with a wing commander and some other officer in it. I said, 'Sorry, boys, they got me!' which must have sounded awful silly. They laughed and told me to get in, and drove me off to the hospital.

"I was operated on that afternoon. They fished a piece of explosive cannon shell out of my hip, from right up against the bone.

"That evening Rickey came around to see me. He told me that the bomber I attacked had gone down in flames and was officially credited to me. Was I glad!

"That was on Saturday, and of course you know the Japs landed on Singapore Island the following Monday. You can imagine how I felt lying there in the hospital, with them coming! Then Tuesday night and Wednesday morning I could tell by the artillery fire that they were getting close. I never felt so helpless. There was a big gun only a little way from the hospital. It started working early Wednesday morning, making a terrific racket, shaking the building every time it went off. Then, what was much worse, the bombers started coming after this gun, some of their bombs just missing the hospital. It was terrifying.

"About midmorning on Wednesday we heard rifle and machine-gun fire just outside the hospital. I figured this was the finish. I had an orderly bring my revolver, because I was going to shoot myself when the Japs came in.

"All at once Doc M— came running into the ward where I was, all out of breath. 'How do you feel?' he asked me. 'Not so bad,' I told him.

"Then he said, 'Would you like to take a chance on a ship?' Boy, I felt like a drowning man grabbing a life preserver. 'Would I ever!' I said.

"'Well,' he asked me, 'can you walk?'

"'Sure,' I answered, and I jumped out of bed to show him and promptly collapsed on the floor. My leg wouldn't do a thing. Then I saw a broom in a corner and got it and managed to hobble around the room a little, using it for a crutch. He looked pretty dubious but finally said I could come along.

"The other fellows in my ward were all too badly off to be moved. I'll never forget the look of utter despair in their eyes when I last saw them as I was going out.

"There were five of us that the doc had collected. We all got into an ambulance that was full of shrapnel holes and had its windows smashed, and we drove off.

"On the way into town we had to stop because of a bombing raid. The doc, who had been riding in front, came around in back to encourage us, but he seemed more scared than we were. We could see his teeth chattering. One stick of bombs dropped in a line right across us. I could see the first three explosions coming towards us, the third one real close. Then the fourth landed the other side of us!

"After that was over we drove on as near as we could get to the docks. The doc was taking a chance on being able to squeeze us onto a medium-sized merchant ship that was getting ready to leave. We had to walk about half a mile to the dock. I was using that broom for a crutch; and no kidding, I was just sweating with agony when I got there.

"We were in luck. There was still room for us. I got put in the Fourth Assistant Engineer's cabin, along with an R.A.F. engineer officer who had lost one eye, so we called him 'One-Eyed-Ike.' There were more than two thousand people on board, mostly European civilians, men, women, and children. It was a refrigerated ship, and they turned off the refrigerating machinery so that some of the people could stay down in the hold. The rest had to stay on deck, except for a few of the wounded who were given the ship's officers' cabins.

"About six o'clock that evening the ship pulled away from the dock and anchored outside the harbor. Then about seven o'clock next morning we sailed, in convoy with another merchant ship, with a light cruiser for escort.

"We got our first attack about ten o'clock that morning. Several of us were chatting together, talking about how lucky we were to get away, when the call was passed along, 'Enemy aircraft approaching.'

"After that there was pandemonium. A big bunch of planes, mostly dive-bombers, came over and most of them made for our ship because it was biggest. We were in narrow waters yet so the ship couldn't maneuver to avoid the bombs, and they fell all around us, shaking the ship and almost lifting it out of the water sometimes. Each time after a close one we listened for the sound of the ship's engines. We knew as long as they kept running we weren't hit seriously, and boy, they were running so hard they sounded as though they were coming right up through the deck! I heard afterwards that during this attack they got three knots more out of the ship than she had ever been able to do before!

"The gun crews on deck were wonderful. They let off with everything they had at every plane as it came over — pom-poms, Lewis guns. Tommy guns. There were even chaps firing with rifles and revolvers. They got two bombers definitely destroyed and three probables out of thirty-some planes that attacked us.

"One small bomb came through the roof of a cabin about ten yards from ours and exploded, killing the fellows in there. The concussion knocked an electric fan off the wall in our cabin. It fell on One-Eyed-Ike, who was lying face down on the floor, and I had to laugh because it lay there on top of him, still running, as if it was getting electricity from him! The bomb started a fire, but they called for volunteers and got it out in a little while.

"Two chaps were brought into our cabin to die who had been on a gun post that got hit by another small bomb. They were so mangled that they had to be carried in blankets. The blood was soaking through the blankets and running all over, and the nurses gave the men morphia to ease them out.

"The nurses were wonderful and shielded the patients with their bodies each time the bombs fell. Most of the bombers machine-gunned us as they passed over, but they didn't cause many casualties. One fellow got a bullet that went right through his chest from front to back without hitting any vital spot. They just covered up the two holes and he was all right.

"After this attack we had a two-hour respite, and by the time the next one started we were out in open water where the ship could maneuver. I had been moved down then to the bottom of the hold, so I couldn't tell what was going on myself but the others told me what happened. It was a high-level attack by sixty-seven planes, and it lasted for more than two hours. We received most of the attention, just as before.

"Each plane dropped its bombs in a stick after a careful run. The captain was credited by all with saving the ship, for he kept watching the bombers through his binoculars, and each time one came up on its bombing run, and he saw its bomb doors swing open, he'd call out, 'Hard a-port!' or 'Hard a-starboard!' and the ship would turn as sharply as it could— which was just enough to mess up the aim.

"One stick of them went off so close to us that the bombs lifted the ship way up, almost clear out of the water, and damaged it some. Another lot were much closer yet, just grazing the ship's side, and would have blown in the whole side of the ship and sunk us, but they all failed to go off. Either it was a miracle or the pilot forgot to fuse his bombs. There were many more near misses, too.

"It was tough on us down below, because we didn't know what was happening or when the next ones were coming. We could hear and feel the explosions. Each time we'd listen for the sound of the engines afterwards, and when we heard them we knew we were still all right.

"Finally it was over and we were still going strong. Most of the passengers had been on the top deck all the time, and had spent the time singing hymns and songs to keep from going nuts. Now that it was over they all had a communal prayer of thanksgiving, and then took up a collection to buy a plaque for the ship in commemoration of all this. They raised about twenty-five hundred Singapore dollars and gave it to the Captain, who made a little speech of thanks.

"We had no more attacks after that, and next day we arrived in Batavia. I got off and was hobbling along the wharf planning to get to a hospital when an army doctor came along and said to me, 'Why don't you get aboard that hospital ship docked over there? Then when they sail you'll be all set.' So I did as he suggested, and here I am!"

So ended Stewie's adventurous escape to fight again.

Chapter X

War over the Jungle

To go back to where I left off at the end of Chapter VIII. The four of us in our patched-up airplanes now headed out across the Straits of Malacca. When we were eight or ten miles out I noticed that my engine seemed to be working very hard to keep up with the other machines. Then I realized that I hadn't retracted my wheels yet — I'd been so busy looking back and monkeying with my camera that I had forgotten all about them! I raised them hurriedly, feeling embarrassed and hoping the others hadn't noticed, and my airplane speeded up at once so that I was able to ease my engine considerably.

We'd been warned that our airplanes were in very ropy condition, having been patched up and put together so hastily; and I found this was no exaggeration concerning mine. One of my wheels wouldn't lock in its retracted position and kept dropping down. I had to raise it every couple of minutes. The position indicator light for my wheels wasn't working, so at first I could never tell for sure when this wheel was clear up. Then, noticing a hole in the bottom of my fuselage right by the place where the wheel came up, I found I could tell by the amount of daylight coming through the hole whether it was clear up or not.

My air-speed indicator registered zero at all times, and the airplane was "out of trim" so that I had to keep holding the stick to one side to keep it level. However, the engine purred nicely and the oil pressure and radiator temperature were normal, so I didn't mind the other faults.

Denny also appeared to be having trouble with his landing gear, for one of his wheels kept coming down the same as mine. And Tom, in his Brewster, flew for the first ten or fifteen minutes with both his wheels clear down. His trouble was just that he couldn't find the right gadget to raise them with, not having flown a Brewster before. Brownie seemed to be getting along all right in his Hurricane, although afterwards he said his propeller pitch control wasn't working, so that his engine just ran at any speed it felt like.

Everything went smoothly for the first forty-five minutes, and we were well on our way across the Straits of Malacca. In another fifteen or twenty minutes we should reach the coast of Sumatra, and an hour or so after that would bring us to Palembang.

Then Denny, who was leading us, suddenly began waggling his wings as a sign of distress, and headed downward and left toward an island a few miles in diameter, which we were nearing.

I took over the lead of the remaining three. Denny was obviously planning to force-land on this island, so I followed after him with my three, to see where he landed and whether he made it safely. We circled around above him while he made a couple of passes at a small field in one part of the island; but this seemed to worry him. He came back up alongside me, motioning me to go on, so, regretfully, the three of us headed on southward.

In a few minutes we struck the coast of Sumatra. We had to follow it southward now, until we came to the river Musi leading inland to Palembang, all of which had seemed very simple so far. But I had only followed the coast a short distance before I realized that I might soon be in difficulties.

The crude map which I had picked up in the dispersal hut for emergency was an absolute menace — it showed only the one river going inland, with hardly any details by which I could identify it, whereas there seemed to be fully a dozen rivers leading in from this section of the coast! Picking the right one was going to be a most delicate matter.

To make matters worse the weather was getting bad, with the ceiling down to a thousand feet and thunderstorms and rain scattered all around, so I didn't have the visibility I needed to discern the course of each river. We didn't have enough gas to allow for errors in navigation; if I picked the wrong one we'd be sunk.

There's something frightening about being unsure of your way in an airplane. You can't stop and debate over your map as to which is the right way before going on. You're going, and fast, whether you've decided which way to go or not, and whether you're headed right or wrong, so your decisions are forced. I had terrible thoughts of our three precious fighter planes lost and crashing in the jungle somewhere, the result of my faulty map reading.

One after another I passed up these rivers, each one because it didn't seem to check with the one on my map from what I could see of it, until I had gone by several and it seemed I surely must have gone far enough. I began to wonder helplessly if one of those I'd passed up had been the right one, and if so how I'd ever be able to find which it was if I went back now.

Then out of the rain and mist ahead another appeared which seemed to take the right direction in from the coast, curving like the one on my map, so I turned inland on it, praying I wasn't making a mistake. Within a few minutes I saw a couple of steamers on it, so I thought I must be right. And a little farther on we came in sight of Palembang itself. I gave one of my biggest sighs of relief!

There was a large storm raging to the north of town where the airdrome is located, but in view of our limited gasoline supply I decided not to wait for the storm to pass over. The jungle airdrome where I had landed before on the way from Java up to Singapore was only about fifty miles southwest from Palembang, and as the weather looked good in that direction I led on towards it. I wanted to get my three machines down safely and as quickly as possible, and I didn't care where!

A few minutes more, following the little old-fashioned railway (Sumatra's only one, I believe) that twisted and curved roughly southwest from Palembang, and we were circling to land.

As I was taxiing towards the watch office, I thought how much had happened in the two weeks since I landed here before, when the American Army Flying Fortress was here. It seemed a much longer time.

The weather at Palembang was reported to be worsening, so we stayed overnight. We were anxious for news of 300 Squadron, because of the dismaying rumors that we'd heard while in Singapore, and I questioned everyone I met to see what I could find out. No one seemed to know definitely how they had fared, although all agreed that they must have had hard fighting as Palembang had been raided heavily. One or two had heard rumors that the squadron were wiped out completely.

Next morning, with our airplanes refueled, we flew back and landed at Palembang. A man drove out in a car to meet me and point to where I should park my machine, and

I saw it was Squadron Leader T—. At least he was all right, I thought thankfully. He picked us up in his car and drove us into town, where we met several more of the boys in the hotel where they were staying. It was a joyful reunion, everybody shaking hands and shouting and pounding each other on the back. We hadn't known which of them to expect to see alive and they hadn't known what had become of us.

They weren't wiped out by any means, but they'd lost most of their airplanes. They'd had very heavy attacks for three days running, fighting against vastly superior numbers — the enemy capitalizing on their shortage of aircraft by sending successive raids one right after the other. In this way they sometimes caught the boys while they were on the ground refueling and rearming after one battle and were able to destroy some of their machines on the ground.

A lot of the boys had gone missing, but several turned up again after having bailed out or force-landed in the jungle and made their way back. Kleck, however, was among those definitely killed.

175 Squadron were operating here now, with the eight Hurricanes they had brought down from Singapore two days before. Some of our own planes which had been slightly damaged were just about ready to go again, and the boys hoped to start operating a few machines themselves in another day. Several were absent, having gone down to Java to pick up some new Hurricanes and bring them here. Three or four were now resting up from exposure and minor injuries from getting shot down and finding their way back here. They had some rather wild stories to tell.

Cam, for example, had been shot down and had crashed in heavy jungle a long way from Palembang, but managed to extricate himself from the wreck quite unhurt, though shaken. Some natives came around soon, appearing reason- ably friendly, and they indicated that they'd take him to civilization in return for the gasoline in his tanks. Considering this quite a bargain, he wrote out a slip of paper, saying they could have all the gasoline they found, and gave it to them. None of them could read, but they seemed to trust him all right.

They were very interested in the wrecked Hurricane, climbing all over it and inspecting it carefully. Cam was afraid that sooner or later one of them might accidentally fire the guns. He spent quite a while trying to show them by signs that they mustn't meddle with the firing button. He says he gathered them all around and then acted as though he were going to press the button, then shook his head and waved his hands, saying, "Bad! Very bad! Mustn't do!" He repeated the performance until he was sure they had the idea. Then he started off with those who were to take him to safety.

They made their way to a river where they got into canoes and paddled off, but their progress was very slow and constantly interrupted. About every half hour the natives would meet some friends in other canoes, whereupon they'd stop and all pile into each other's boats and sit cross-legged, jabbering to each other, for an hour or so. His rescuers would point at him and jabber to their friends and laugh, saying what sounded to him like, "Look what we've got! Isn't he funny?" And he would beam back at them. He said he felt called upon to sit cross-legged, too.

He said, "I'd made signs that I was thirsty, and one of them would say, 'Thirsty? All right— have a drink!'— or what sounded like it. Then he'd take a gourd and scoop up some filthy muddy water out of the river and give it to me!"

Frequently they'd stop at some native village along the river and go ashore for a visit, all sitting cross-legged and jabbering by the hour, while Cam smiled at everyone and tried to look interested. Meals were gourds of rice, so filthy it made him sick to his stomach.

After four days of this kind of travel they arrived at a village where he was able to get in touch with the outside world by a radio set. He was told to stay where he was, and soon a Dutch Army car arrived— the village was connected with the outside world by a road of sorts— and he was driven back to Palembang. He was still quite weak and shaken from his ordeal when we met him.

Mac also had a bizarre experience. He had been out on a shipping escort with Junior, and on their way back they ran into twelve Navy Zero fighters. Junior was never heard of again. Mac got chased into some clouds, and when he came out he found himself totally lost. When nearly out of gas he picked a swamp close to a river and force-landed there. All fighter pilots are now provided with little collapsible rubber dinghies (boats), packed into their parachute cushions, and Mac took his and made his way to the river. There he unpacked and inflated it, climbed in, and started paddling downstream.

These dinghies aren't built for speed, and Mac found his progress very slow. Presently he saw a canoe tied to the shore with no one in attendance and paddled over to it. He couldn't find anyone around, so he pinned a ten guilder note to a near-by tree in payment and paddled off in his new purchase. After a time he met up with some natives in canoes, who escorted him to a village near-by, where he was shown to the chief's house. There to his amazement, right in the heart of the jungle, he was treated to ice-cold beer from a refrigerator and put up in a huge room with the biggest and most luxurious bed he'd ever seen!

He stayed there for a couple of days, living elegantly on imported European foods, which the progressive-minded chief kept in stock, until he was rescued.

Not all the stories were pleasant. The saddest was that of Roy K—, a very young Canadian sergeant pilot, from Toronto. Vic, who was Roy's flight commander, told me about it that evening after dinner in the hotel where we boarded, while we sat toying with our coffee and watching the funny little wall lizards on the high ceiling of the dining room go about their trade of keeping the mosquitoes and other insects cleaned up.

I wish I could reproduce Vic's words the way he told it, speaking slowly and haltingly, his voice starting to quaver once or twice, pausing occasionally to get control, his eyes blinking and watching the ceiling, avoiding mine. For Roy was a wonderful kid and Vic had been his very close friend.

He told me that Roy was wounded in the leg during a battle. His airplane was shot up badly, but he managed to get back and land all right. Then while he was taxiing across the field his damaged machine caught fire. The gas tank must have been holed, for it was all ablaze in an instant; and because of his wounded leg Roy had trouble getting out. By the time he got clear he was badly burned about the face, legs, and arms.

He was taken to the Dutch hospital at Palembang, where he seemed to do all right for the first twenty-four hours. Then shock set in and he started weakening. Vic went to see him as often as he could get time. He visited him about eight o'clock in the morning on the third day, promising to be back again at four in the afternoon. Something told him that morning that all was not well, for the doctors were letting Roy have morphia to ease the pain, something they had refused him before.

Vic was very busy that day and was delayed slightly in the afternoon, so he didn't arrive at the hospital until a few minutes past four. There he found, to his grief, that Roy had just passed away.

The sisters told him that Roy held on desperately until four, waiting for him to come, because he wanted so badly for Vic to be with him when he died. But when Vic didn't arrive on time his strength gave out. Just before he passed away he looked around at the sisters and begged, "Someone please hold my hand and call me 'Roy' before I die!" One of the sisters took his hand and called him "Roy," and that was how he died, halfway around the world from his home in Toronto.

The weather in Sumatra was hot and stifling as before, little local thunderstorms occasionally breaking the heat for short periods, after which the sun would come out brighter and hotter than ever and the air would be stifling again, heavy with moisture from the steaming ground. We speculated a lot on how long it would be before the enemy tried to take Sumatra, and we weren't to be long in finding out.

The morning of the day after I arrived at Palembang the raid sirens sounded just before breakfast. A few of our boys were already out at the airdrome, doing readiness with what machines we had serviceable, along with 175 Squadron. Those of us who weren't on duty drove out to the drome to see what was going on.

We found that our boys and all of 175 Squadron were flying. The fellows on ground duty said that some Navy Zeros had been over about half an hour before and all our planes had gone off after them. They and the Navy Zeros had disappeared, so presumably our boys were chasing them somewhere.

The ground chaps were very concerned about a Hurricane they had seen shot down. They didn't know who the pilot was. It had been approaching to land, they said, with its wheels and flaps down, when two Navy Zeros dived on it. The first one, in pulling out of its dive, snapped its wings and crashed, but the second one shot the Hurricane down. Some thought they'd seen the pilot bail out, but no one knew yet. At present some low clouds over the airdrome obscured all view of what was going on above, but we could hear no noise.

Just then Scotty, a big husky chap from Alberta, walked into the dispersal building— and what a Scotty! It was he who had been piloting the Hurricane that was shot down. He had escaped by a miracle, bailing out at less than five hundred feet, and landing in the jungle a mile or so away. He was dirtied and dishevelled and still very dazed, wearing an expression on his face as if he'd just fallen out of bed!

He had just arrived from Java, ferrying a new Hurricane for the squadron. Quite a reception! It was too bad that his machine was lost so quickly, but it cost the enemy an airplane and pilot both, so we couldn't call it a bad trade.

After a few minutes we heard airplanes droning somewhere overhead, hidden from the airdrome by the low broken clouds. Occasionally there was the quick crisp roll of a burst of machine-gun fire in the sky, with more droning about and the sound of first one engine and then another power-diving.

As we had nothing to do at the drome we decided to get away from it before any bombing started, and we walked up the road a couple of hundred yards, sat down on a grassy bank, and awaited developments. We hadn't long to wait, for we suddenly found ourselves flat in the roadside ditch as if drawn there by magic, while the anti-aircraft guns went berserk at a single bomber that was approaching at about four hundred feet, beneath the low clouds.

It let go a stick of four bombs and we counted the earth-shaking booms, one after another, each one closer to us. Then the bomber was passing over the road and we cowered low in case they tried to machine-gun us. As soon as it was a safe distance away and the guns were chasing it up into the clouds on the other side of the drome I rose half out of the ditch and got a snapshot of the huge white clouds of smoke from the bombs as they drifted across the road about a hundred yards away. All four bombs had fallen well outside the airdrome— the poorest bombing I have ever seen, considering the low altitude from which they were dropped.

There seemed to be a lot more fighters and bombers around, but the low clouds fooled them so they couldn't find the airdrome. After milling around a few more minutes they all cleared away, and our fighters on patrol came back and landed. As I remember, they had shot down two or three bombers during the melee, and 175 Squadron had one pilot missing.

After they got refueled Brownie and I volunteered to go on readiness for a couple of the boys who had been flying. The two of us had a scramble about midmorning, but the flight proved uneventful, as the approaching enemies turned away before reaching Palembang. We stayed up for a while, doing a standing patrol at high altitude for more than an hour in hope that they'd change their minds and come back, but the activity seemed to have ceased for the morning.

After we landed, someone else took our places and I spent the afternoon in town, doing some shopping and getting my quarters fixed up. We took our meals in the Luxor Hotel and slept across the street in what had been a sort of rooming house, but was now turned over to us. We had to furnish our own quarters.

I had a cot, but no mosquito net for it, and as that is most important in Sumatra it was the first thing I attended to that afternoon. I got a net and then started looking around for wires to stretch it over. While I was working on my net, a little Malayan fellow came around who did our laundry, and was a particularly good scout, always trying to be helpful. As soon as he saw what I was doing he started jabbering vehemently, picked up my camp cot and tossed it out of the room.

Then he scurried away and presently appeared carrying a small wooden bed, complete with mattress, which he triumphantly deposited where my cot had been! Then he jabbered some more and hustled away again, to reappear with some boards and a hammer. Still jabbering happily and working frenziedly he put up a framework for my mosquito netting in a matter of minutes. I gave him a guilder, which of course made him happier than ever, though in his case I think he'd have done it for nothing.

After that I went around town doing some shopping, getting my Singapore money changed into guilders Dutch (East Indies dollars), and cabling my folks back home that I was safely out of Singapore.

Instead of rickshas, in Palembang they had a queer sort of tricycle conveyance which the coolie rode on and pedaled. You sat in a wide seat, over the axle, which carried two passengers. This seemed to be quite an improvement over rickshas.

Most of us took in a movie that night, in the theatre next door to the hotel. You might say there was something prophetic about the picture in a reverse way. The title was "He Stayed for Breakfast." Most of us didn't.

Chapter XI

The Battle of Palembang

From what I have since seen of the newspapers published at this time, I gather that the Battle of Palembang did not receive a great deal of prominence in the news, although it represented a major step in the enemy's conquest of the Far East — the main step between Singapore and Java. The final stages of the now-certain fall of Singapore were still occurring when Palembang was attacked, and I presume the eyes of the world were still on Singapore.

We ourselves, realizing that the Singapore show was all over but the shouting and that Sumatra was the obvious next battle zone, were "digging in" in our own way, ferrying up new aircraft from Java and getting damaged ones repaired, in anticipation of the blow. Alas, we had little time, and the blow came even before Singapore had surrendered!

I was on dawn readiness next morning, which was Saturday, February 14th — a gloomy, misty sort of morning, with sullen hangings of low cloud drifting across the airdrome. Tudor, our engineer officer (chief mechanic), and his men had been doing themselves proud in getting damaged machines repaired and new replacement machines fixed for combat. As a result, we had eight airplanes in 300 Squadron that morning, less than a week from the time the squadron's equipment had been virtually wiped out. 175 Squadron had gotten some new airplanes also, and I believe they had a full twelve that morning. Anyway, there were enough Hurricanes dispersed around the held at readiness to make an imposing show after what our squadrons had been through. When the light improved I got up on the nose of my airplane and took a snapshot of part of the array.

Towards nine o'clock both squadrons were scrambled and sent out together on a patrol over the Banka Straits, a hundred miles or so northeast. We spent half or three-quarters of an hour out there uneventfully, flying among and above tumbled masses of low broken cloud beneath a thick sullen overcast. A Jap invasion fleet was supposed to be approaching, so we heard; but it apparently hadn't got this far at least, for we saw no ships.

Our C.O. who was leading the formation finally called it a day and led us back towards Palembang. As we neared the city we had to come down through a lot of cloud, and in doing so our formation got broken up so that when we came underneath, the two squadrons were separated.

I was leading a pair to the left and behind the C.O. Looking back I could see several machines a couple of miles behind, and one of them seemed to be diving toward another that was lower down. I was just a little suspicious, not enough to call out a warning, but keeping my eye on what was going on back there, until it was too late. Four long thin white lines suddenly reached out ahead from the plane that was diving, converging on the one in front of it — tracers — and then the one in front dived away leaving a thick trail of steam and glycol smoke!

Someone was calling, "Look out— bandits!" and someone else called, "Tally-Ho!" Everything seemed to be in confusion back there, a melee of airplanes milling around, while we in front wheeled and headed back towards them. My number two broke away to chase after something he saw. A few seconds later I looked back to see a Navy Zero diving down on me, his big stubby round nose and silver-colored propeller-spinner identifying him as enemy even at quite a distance. Another was following him. I opened my throttle and swung around hard to face him. I was facing him before he could get within firing range and I thought it was going to be a head-on show, both of us coming straight at each other, shooting, seeing who would give way first before we collided; but he didn't seem to want that now that he'd lost his chance for surprise. Before we were within firing range of each other he zoomed up away. His partner behind did likewise. They had all the advantage of height and speed, so there was nothing I could do about it, and I lost track of them.

There were several airplanes milling around an area two or three miles across and I joined in, intercepting different ones that all turned out to be Hurricanes when I got close enough for identification. The Navy Zeros appeared to have all left, and the skirmish was over.

It was just then that Control began broadcasting a rather unusual order: "Hello, all Tiger and Evitt aircraft! All Tiger and Evitt aircraft! Don't land at your base! Do not land at your base! Go and land at B Airdrome. Land at B Airdrome!"

B Airdrome was the jungle airdrome southwest of Palembang. I couldn't understand why we were being sent there, but presumed that our own field was bombed and unserviceable. I headed down the railway from Palembang and soon reached B Airdrome and landed as ordered.

After parking my machine I made my way to the watch office to join the crowd of other 175 and 300 Squadron pilots gathering there, and to hear the startling news: The reason we were ordered down here was that Palembang Airdrome was surrounded by more than two hundred parachutists, dropped there while we were away on our patrol!

And we'd wondered when the attack on Sumatra would come!

No one could learn anything very definite. The situation was supposed to be confused, with fighting going on around the drome and the city. Telephone communication with the airdrome was dead.

Towards noon B Airdrome's Operations called for someone to do a reconnaissance to Palembang, studying the traffic along the highway to see if there were any signs of Jap troop movements down the road in our direction. I offered to go, as reco work was somewhat in my line, and it was a relief to get off the ground after the tension of waiting around for something to happen.

I scouted the road all the way, flying just above the tree-tops and getting lost once or twice by taking the wrong turns while flying in the rain, but didn't see anything that looked like military traffic coming.

There were dozens of motor cars streaming down the road. Apparently all the civilians were getting out at high speed. I could see white shirts and colored dresses in the cars, so I knew they couldn't be Japs.

At Palembang the only indication I could see of how the fighting was going was that the Dutch had set fire to some of their big oil storage tanks, which seemed a bad sign. There was the familiar sight of frightening red flames, with angry black smoke pumping skyward and drifting over the city, nearly hiding it. It would have awed me if I hadn't come so recently from Singapore.

I returned and gave in my report, which relieved everyone because they had feared that the Japs might be attacking here right away, and we spent the rest of the day at readiness.

I was very worried about my belongings, which were all left behind in my room at Palembang, so I got to work on the telephone. After a time I managed to get the Palembang exchange and finally got through to our rooming house there. Who should answer the telephone but Red! He hadn't been flying that morning, and consequently was among those left behind.

He said he didn't know just how the situation stood, but thought it was pretty bad. No, the Japs weren't inside the town, but he thought they were close around. He and Mac and a couple of others were getting ready to leave up the river in a motor boat. I asked him to try to bring a little writing case, in which I had stuffed my most priceless possessions in case of just such an emergency.

It was in a small traveling bag which I had packed with my next most valuable belongings, and he said he'd try to bring the bag and all.

Good old Red! I have never seen or heard of him since, but I've got that bag all right, thanks to him. It reached me more than two months later, Red having got it to Java and then given it to others who were leaving for India, as he stayed to fight to the last. Nearly all the films I took in Singapore were in it.

Towards evening some of our ground personnel began arriving from Palembang with the news that the battle was apparently lost, though the city was still in our hands when they left.

I think this is where I should bring in the story of Mickey N—, one of our pilots who was on the ground at Palembang Airdrome when the parachutists landed. He saw much of the battle, with experiences nearly as hair-raising as any he'd encountered in the air.

Mickey was the youngest pilot of our squadron. He had been hurt slightly in a crash a few days before and, being temporarily off flying, was doing the ground job of "Airdrome Control Pilot" that morning. This meant he had to stay on the airdrome looking after incoming and outgoing planes, taking telephone calls, and generally being on hand to take the blame for anything that went wrong. Like Stewie, he also told me his story on the hospital ship two or three weeks later:

"You remember when you fellows took off that morning to go out over the Banka Straits? Well, some time after you left a big bunch of bombers appeared from the north, flying very low. We thought we were in for a real pasting, but instead of bombing the drome they just circled it.

"Then we saw that they were dropping parachutists over the jungle, scores of them, in a big circle all around the drome, about a mile outside it.

"I thought we were in an awful spot, because they had us completely surrounded, and I expected they'd be closing in on us right away. I rang up Operations and told them what had happened so they could warn you not to land back there; a little while later the phone was dead.

"Several squadron leaders and wing commanders were there at the time, and they got all the personnel organized to defend the place. We took up positions along the road which skirts the west side of the drome in two or three buildings there and braced ourselves for the attack which we all thought would begin in a matter of minutes. I suppose there were a couple hundred of us all told, including the ground personnel of our squadrons who were on duty. Nothing happened for a while. There wasn't a sound from the jungle, and we kept getting more and more tense as time went by.

"Pretty soon we saw you chaps coming back from your patrol over the Banka Straits. We could see some airplanes milling around in the distance and heard several bursts of machine-gun fire, so we knew you must be having a scrap of some kind. Then one Hurricane came in, streaming glycol smoke, and landed. That was Ting. He had his radiator shot up, and said he'd been jumped by a couple of Navy Zeros. Then we saw most of you heading off southwest, having heard Control, I suppose, warning you not to land here.

"But then we saw that two Hurricanes were coming back. They came in and landed. I expected to see them picked off by snipers from the jungle while they were taxiing back up the runway, for they were right out in the open of course. However, nothing happened. I ran out to tell them to get going, but by the time I got to the pilots they'd already stopped their engines and were climbing out of their cockpits. They were Bertie and Kelly. They hadn't heard the warning not to land here, and when I told them what had happened you should have seen them move. You never in your life saw two chaps get back into their machines and take off so quick!

"Then, horror of horrors, right when we expected to see Japs coming out of the jungle at any moment, in came four Hurricanes and landed! They were new reinforcements for us, being ferried up from Java, and of course they had no radios installed so they couldn't hear any warning. As soon as they landed some of us piled into a car and tore out onto the field to warn the pilots. We told them to turn around and take off as fast as they could and go down to B Airdrome, but they all said they couldn't. They didn't have enough gas. They'd had bad weather all the way up which made them fly around a lot, and their tanks were almost empty.

"So there was nothing for it but to get a petrol tanker out on the field and fill them up, hoping we had time. You know how the jungle comes right up to the airdrome on all sides there, so you can imagine how conspicuous we felt working out in the open on those Hurricanes, knowing there were a couple hundred or more Japs with rifles and tommy-guns in that jungle! We fairly tore around, and we got those four Hurricanes refueled in what I bet was an all-time record. Were we relieved to see them safely away again and to get back under cover!

"Some army officers came around after a time and inspected our positions and gave us advice. They had their headquarters back about a mile or so along the road to Palembang. We asked them if they'd made any contact with the enemy yet and they said no, except for shooting a few while they were coming down in their parachutes. They hadn't seen anything of them yet, and thought they might be infiltrating down towards Palembang, which was eight or ten miles away.

"We waited and waited and nothing happened, and the tension of just sitting there not knowing what to expect or when to expect it was almost as bad as being attacked and having it out. Finally a couple of the army officers came to tell us they had orders to retire to Palembang, to defend the city, and they advised us to do likewise. With our telephone wires cut, we couldn't get in touch with Operations for orders, and we decided to take their advice.

"There were lots of cars and lorries to go, and I caught a ride with an army doctor. We started off ahead of most of the rest and drove along without incident for the first two or three miles. Then we rounded a corner and saw a couple of wrecked cars in the road about a quarter of a mile ahead.

"'Oh, oh!' the doc says. 'This looks like an ambush!' He put on the brakes, and just then there was a terrific explosion in front of the windshield and I felt something stab into my neck. Next thing I knew I was lying face down in the road, coughing and gagging on blood in my throat and mouth, with blood all over my clothes, too. The explosion must have been a hand grenade.

"I thought sure I was dying. I couldn't talk or breathe or do anything except gag on blood that kept flowing into my throat as well as outside, from my wound, and I expected that if I didn't die the Japs would be along in a minute and shoot me anyway.

"But nothing happened right away, and after a bit my ears stopped ringing so much and I was conscious of a voice calling me in a loud whisper: 'Hey! Come on and get down in this ditch — quick!' It was the doc calling me. I opened my eyes and saw I was a few feet from a ditch at the side of the road. I gathered all my strength and half leaped and half fell over into it and huddled down by the doc. The ditch was about three feet deep.

"I still thought I was dying. The blood in my throat made a rattling sound when I breathed, and I remembered the phrase about death rattling in one's throat, and thought that was it. The doc must have thought so, too, for he kept reaching over and feeling my pulse.

"In a few minutes we heard another car coming. It stopped a few yards up the road from ours and we heard the occupants scrambling out and making for the ditch. Then pretty soon we heard the Japs coming out of the jungle and onto the road, and I thought, 'Now it's coming!'

"We heard them talking and heard their footsteps on the road, and then they came up to our car, which was only three feet from the edge of the ditch we were in! They walked all around it, jabbering to each other, opening and shutting the doors, and apparently giving it a general once-over. I knew it would come now, because it could only be a matter of seconds before one of them glanced down and saw us, and I was trying my best to look like I was dead, lying with my mouth open and the wound in my neck showing. Once one of them jumped right across the ditch without noticing us. I just couldn't believe it when I heard them walk away after a little while.

"However, they didn't go far, and they kept coming back. It was evident they were taking up stations around here for the time being, for they kept walking up and down the road and in and out of the jungle and all around, jabbering back and forth to each other. Then one of them standing near us in the road called out excitedly and several others came running, and my blood froze! 'Now they have found us,' I thought. But it wasn't us. It was two other fellows a few yards up along the ditch from where we were — the ones who'd scrambled out of the car that came after us. They put two bullets into each of them, and after each report there was a sickening 'oof!' from the one who was hit. Then at the last report the doc himself moaned and jerked, and I thought they were shooting us now, but he'd just done it involuntarily.

"Pretty soon we heard a lorry coming. It stopped a little way up the road. We heard the door open and the driver getting out, and then his voice, pleading, 'Don't shoot me, you! Don't shoot me!'

"Then a shot, and silence.

"It began to rain, and all I thought was, 'Thank God! A little concealment!' But it stopped again soon.

"After a time some Japs came along in a Dutch armored car they'd captured. It stopped near us and there was lots of jabbering and running about, and then we heard it drive up and start pushing against our car. It was pushing it sideways, towards us, and we thought they were pushing it into the ditch, which would mean it would fall right on us. But they stopped pushing it when the wheels were just on the edge of the ditch. Apparently they just wanted room enough to get by. Another three inches and it would have toppled in on us.

"Finally, after we'd lain there for over two hours, we heard machine-gun and rifle fire from up the road and bullets whining overhead, and striking around. The Japs withdrew from around us down the road a way. For a time we were in a no man's land between the two fires, but finally our forces got to where we were, and we were able to come out of our cover.

"Our forces were composed of soldiers and R.A.F. chaps from the drome, at the head of a long column of lorries and cars, making their way toward Palembang. The going the rest of the way was slow and we were almost continually under fire. The Japs kept falling back and making ambushes and machine-gunning the road, and there were lots of casualties on both sides. Every little way there were bodies of Japs and British soldiers and airmen, frightful things to look at the way some were torn and mutilated by the bullets, so that it nearly made me sick.

"Eventually we made it into Palembang, where we found the streets packed with cars, lorries, and ambulances around the landing for the ferry on which they had to cross the river to travel south. It would have been a wonderful target for bombers, but fortunately the Dutch had fired their big oil storage tanks and the wind blew the smoke right over the city, hiding everything. I got my wound dressed, and the doc said there was a piece of shrapnel lodged inside my throat. I could only talk in a whisper. I stayed in Palembang overnight with some of the fellows, and we started south next morning."

Such was the adventure that Mickey was having while we were waiting at B Airdrome and wondering what was happening at Palembang!

A wing commander had another interesting little adventure that afternoon, in which he saved himself from capture by the greatest of coolness and quick thinking.

This wing commander was also at Palembang Airdrome when the parachutists arrived, and he didn't leave with the convoy which Mickey told about that fought its way down the road to Palembang. Instead, he stayed at the airdrome until quite late in the afternoon and then, accompanied by another officer, started out down the road in his car.

They had only traveled a couple of miles when they saw several Japs ahead in the road, and stopped. The Japs motioned them to get out of the car and approach, and they did so, covered by rifles and revolvers. One of the Japs was an officer, and when the two R.A.F. officers reached him he said, "You surrender. You my prisoners!"

Quick as a shot the wing commander came back at him. "Surrender, hell! You surrender! I've got two hundred men right back here on the airdrome. You haven't a chance!" (The truth was that there wasn't a man left on the airdrome, and the two officers were entirely alone.)

This took the Japanese officer a little aback, and he began to dicker, insisting that he had many more than two hundred men and it was useless for the British to fight. While this was going on the wing commander noticed out of the corner of his eye that some other Japs were stealing along through the jungle beside the road to get behind him.

"Here!" he admonished the Japanese officer sternly, pointing at the men in the jungle. "You call those men back!" The other meekly obeyed, calling out to the men in Japanese, and they came back.

The dickering continued. The Jap officer was anxious to get the wing commander to surrender his men without fighting. The wing commander appeared to be taken in and talked terms with him, cautiously leading up to his master stroke.

Then, when he had got all the terms the Japs would offer him for surrender he said: "All right. You wait here and I'll go back and talk to my men, to see if they'll agree."

The Jap officer consented. The two R.A.F. officers walked back to their car, got in and turned around, and drove off towards the airdrome. Needless to say, they didn't stop there, not in fact until they were some fifty miles farther up in Central Sumatra, where they turned and made their way to the coast by roads that gave Palembang a wide berth!

As far as they are concerned, the trusting Japanese officer may still be there, waiting for them.

Chapter XII

A River Massacre and A Frightened Pilot

By that evening the situation looked definitely ominous. Reports from people coming from Palembang itself were not too bad on the whole, although conflicting. Some thought the battle was lost, others that our troops were getting the situation under control. All agreed that the city was still in our hands.

But another development had put a much more sinister aspect on it all. Throughout the afternoon a group of Blenheim and Lockheed bombers had been going out as often as they could return and load up, attacking an enormous troop convoy, escorted by warships, which was approaching from the direction of Singapore!

It was obvious that the parachute landing, which might be got under control, was only a prelude to invasion on a scale vastly larger than our small forces in Sumatra could hope to withstand. From now on our job was to give them everything we had, to gain time for preparations for the defense of Java, their big objective.

Our C.O. attended a conference in the Operations room until late that evening. When he came back he told me I was to lead the six airplanes left in our squadron on a certain operation at dawn, and that on our way back we were to do a reco of Palembang and Palembang Airdrome to see what we could of the situation.

We pilots had crowded in on an already overfilled station and there were no beds for us, so we scrounged as many blankets as we could and slept in the Mess — on the floors, on tables, and on chairs, each according to his preference.

I had a rather bad night of it, as I usually do when I have a particular operation planned for the morning, because I can't keep it out of the back of my mind, and so I go to sleep thinking about it. Then after I've been asleep awhile, at the time when one's normal defenses are way down and nerves and feelings all bared and sensitive, the dread sets in and all the dangers seem vivid and terrifying. After Singapore my nerves weren't at their best anyway.

I'd arranged for Operations to ring the telephone in the Mess at five a.m. to waken me, and through the dark night, in the sort of semi-slumber that I experienced between nightmares and wakeful moments thinking of the approaching invasion fleet and of our task at dawn, I seemed to see the telephone glowing in the darkness, menacingly, penetrating into my sleep.

Once when I awoke from a nightmare, shuddering from cold as well as from fright, I realized that it was storming and a cold wind with rain was blowing in on me through the open sides of the building; so I moved off the table I was sleeping on and spent the rest of the night on the floor in a more sheltered place.

It was still pitch-dark when the phone rang, and I stumbled to my feet to answer it dreamily. Five o'clock, time to get down to the field and get our airplanes ready. I roused the boys who were to go with me on the operation, and we stumbled sleepily out of the Mess and trudged along the damp sticky roads to the drome. The rain was over, the sky just beginning to grey in the east, so that we could discern the ghostly outlines of our machines along the edge of the drome. An odd bird or two occasionally called back and forth in the jungle. I felt relieved at being in motion at last, with the knowledge that it would be over soon and then I could relax.

As soon as we reached the watch office I rang up Operations to see if they had any new instructions for me. They told me not to take off yet, but to wait until they phoned back; so after we got our airplanes ready and had our mae wests on we just killed time. Some of the boys found places to lie down and went to sleep.

It was broad daylight before Operations again called to say we could take off and get going. I roused the boys, and in the half-minute's final instructions I gave them I made a remark that was to recoil on me before the day was out. We were to make an attack during which we would have to fly through very heavy anti-aircraft fire, and I told the boys they shouldn't let it worry them — that I didn't think the Japanese anti-aircraft fire was very effective.

How little I knew!

As we taxied out I noticed little wisps of fog among the treetops just outside the airdrome, but I didn't think much about it. There were usually little isolated patches of fog around the countryside here on early mornings. The thick trees on each side of the runway made our position like that of being down in a little canyon, unable to see outside.

Turning at the far end of the runway I gave my engine the gun to take off without waiting for the others to get in formation with me, because I wanted them to take off one at a time. After I left the ground my attention was occupied for a moment by the mechanics of raising my wheels and changing my throttle and propeller pitch settings, so it was not until I was up perhaps a hundred feet that I looked around, and then realized that we were in a terrible jam!

A carpet of fast-forming fog lay all about the countryside and was quickly closing the hole which happened to open over the airdrome!

Hoping desperately that at least part of my formation might still be on the ground I switched on the transmitter and called out, "Don't take off! Do Not take off!" But when I looked back I saw it was too late. There were all five Hurricanes in a long row trailing below and behind me, rising up from the grey blanket that covered the earth in all directions. The airdrome had disappeared completely. This was awful!

I switched on my transmitter again. "Hello, all Evitt aircraft. Wash-out! Wash-out! Land at once; land at once!"

At the same time I turned, dropped my wheels, and throttled back my engine, making for a slight depression in the fog which I hoped marked the airdrome. I was lucky, and when I broke through the bottom of the grey mist I was right over the runway, and I got down O.K.

Then began a nerve-racking half-hour, trying to get the others down. The fog was thin enough so that when they passed directly over they could see down through and spot the drome, but when they got away to make their approaches they, of course, lost sight of it immediately and had to guess where it was. I borrowed a Very pistol and all the available green cartridges from the watch office, and ran out to the middle of the runway. Then every time I heard an airplane approaching the field I'd shoot a cartridge straight up, the little ball of green fire rising and arching over just at the top of the fog, to spot the field for him.

That helped, and soon one of the Hurricanes managed to break into sight more or less over the edge of the field, and by means of a hair-raising vertical turn close to the ground in order to get in line with the runway, and some violent fishtailing to kill his speed, the pilot made it. He came taxiing back, and I saw it was Kelly. He grinned at me and made a motion as if wiping sweat from his forehead. I held up clasped hands in congratulation.

The other four were still droning around up there: first one, then another throttling down and gliding into the fog at a point where he hoped the airdrome was, the sound of his engine breaking out again at full throttle as he zoomed back up after finding he was wrong. Frequently one of them would come close enough for us to see him, but not lined up right to land.

Finally Bertie got down safely, and that made two safe, three to go.

As Bertie was shutting off his engine another Hurricane broke through into sight. It landed on the cross runway at the far side of the field, disappeared behind a slight rise in the ground; then its tail appeared above the rise, poised vertically for an instant, and went on over, and the next minute the fire truck and ambulance went flying across the field in that direction. Two safe, one crashed.

Another got down safely a couple of minutes later, but the last one spent a good fifteen minutes more milling around and making approaches that weren't quite right to bring him in, until finally he made it, too, and I sighed thankfully to see him roll to a stop, undamaged. We lost one machine in the whole affair. For a time I was afraid we were going to lose five.

The ambulance came back from the far side of the field, bringing the pilot of the wrecked airplane. Sergeant F—. He was sitting in front with the driver, bruised and dirtied, but uninjured. He said he had struck a bad soft spot in the field, which made his machine go over on its back.

Ever since the parachutists attacked Palembang the morning before and we landed here, other pilots of both squadrons who hadn't been flying that morning had been making their way down here from Palembang, by car and train, to rejoin us; now each of our two squadrons had enough pilots to man all the airplanes of both. It was decided therefore to pool all the airplanes of both squadrons until we got reinforcements, and change off using them, one squadron operating them half the time and the other the rest of the time.

The fog cleared away about nine o'clock, but it was too late now to carry out the operation I was going to lead, and it was canceled. Then at about ten or eleven a bomber crew, back from a raid on an invasion convoy, reported that a large landing force of enemy troops in barges and small open boats were making their way inland from the Banka Straits, up the River Musi toward Palembang.

This news put everyone in a huddle. The force must be stopped before they reached Palembang, or the show would be over. It was decided to send our Hurricanes out at once. If the enemy were in open boats we should be able to wreak terrible havoc among them with our eight and twelve machine-gun Hurricanes.

175 Squadron were on duty at the time, so they were to make the first sortie, and took off at once. In the meantime we of 300 Squadron hiked back to the Mess to see what we could get to eat before they got back, when we would take over the airplanes to make the next raid.

They returned after an hour or so, all the pilots in great spirits, having had a wonderful show. There had been no enemy fighters to interfere and they had caught the unprotected boats and barges, each crammed tight full with enemy soldiers. It had been a massacre, and they estimated they had killed hundreds.

They recounted lurid details, like seeing some of their victims throw themselves into the air as they were hit, and boats full of dead soldiers sinking, with the water around them red from blood. It gave us some satisfaction to know that these fellows who dealt in horror had got some of their own!

There had been some light anti-aircraft fire from the boats, they said, apparently from machine guns, but only one airplane was hit, and that had only a single bullet hole.

Now it was to be our turn. We took over the airplanes and saw to getting them refueled and rearmed while the 175 Squadron boys went off to lunch. In a short time we were all set, and we started up and taxied to the end of the runway, where we got into squadron formation before taking off. It was the first time we'd taken off in squadron formation since we came to the Far East, as normally the runways were too soft here, or narrow, or damaged by bombs. This runway was good and wide, and the hot sun had dried it. I felt we must be making a magnificent show as we roared up over the boundary of the field all together, and climbed away into the northeast.

Our objective was a hundred miles or so away, and we pulled up to three or four thousand feet, just under a gloomy overcast of heavy cloud. It was a dull murky sky that we flew in, with local rainstorms sitting around the countryside like great white pillars rising from the jungle up to the clouds, so that we appeared to cruise on and on through a great pillared hall — its floor the flat jungle-covered land below, and its ceiling the heavy flat clouds above. Nearing our objective we encountered enormous low cloud formations, detached from the ceiling and drifting independently through our hall; we passed over and through and between their great weird tumbled masses and the vast gloomy caverns in them.

Finally the dull blue-grey water of the Banka Straits appeared ahead, and as we neared the coast we swung northward, until the River Musi appeared ahead of us, winding snake-like inland through the dark carpet of jungle. Somewhere up its course we should find our enemies.

I already had my gunsight turned on and my firing button off safety, for use if we should run into a patrol of Navy Zeros. We were in battle formation, well spread out to guard each other's tails, for it wouldn't be surprising if they had a patrol out guarding the boats this time, after 175 Squadron's devastating attack a couple of hours earlier.

We turned above the mouth of the river and started following upstream; after we'd gone a few miles our C.O. nosed down into a dive and then I saw a few boats parked close to one bank of the river, so tiny in the distance below us that I wondered how he noticed them. It was obviously too small a target for us all to attack at the same time, so I broke away with my number two and did a wide circle, coming around behind the rest. They were shooting the boats up pretty well, so when I got down to them I only put in a short burst from my guns, feeling sure there must be bigger and better game somewhere around.

We climbed up, re-formed, and followed on along the river; and when we'd gone perhaps fifteen or twenty miles farther we found them.

It was the first invasion force I'd ever seen. Boats, scores of them, in a long silent line perhaps two miles from end to end, were strung out parallel to the south bank of the river and a hundred yards or so away from it. From our height it looked like a great venomous snake crawling along the stream. This was one of the moments for which we had been sent halfway around the world!

When we were right above them the C.O. waggled his wings (the signal that we could break formation and go to it) and to each side of me I could see the grey fish-like bellies of Hurricanes turning away to diminish off downwards to the attack.

This seemed to be such a wonderful opportunity that I wanted to make the most of it, so I circled a moment, studying the line of boats and planning my approach. Soon I could see the other Hurricanes far below, like tiny moths floating over the jungle. Then one of them approached the line of boats from one side; as he drew near, his set of delicate white tracers appeared in front of him as if by magic, reaching out ahead and touching one of the boats like a wand, and a cloud of white spray almost completely enveloped it. I had seen twenty or thirty men killed in a twinkling!

I had never seen opportunity like this. Often I had machine-gunned German soldiers, sailors, or airmen on the ground or in ships, but always where they either had a little shelter or concealment, or at least could scatter and throw themselves flat. These fellows had no shelter or concealment except the thin sides of their boats, no better than paper for stopping our bullets, and they were jammed in so tight that they couldn't scatter or throw themselves flat or do anything except just sit up and take it.

Other airplanes followed with their attacks, each in turn approaching one of the boats and raising a mountain of spray around it with his bullets. There were 160 or 240 bullets per second in each of these clouds of spray, depending on whether it was an eight or twelve gun Hurricane. What a massacre!

Now I could see light blue smoke floating away from some of the boats, and I presumed it was from the light anti-aircraft fire which the boys of 175 had reported. Three or four boats were dropping out of line and appeared to be sinking.

My own plans made, I flew eastward, until I was a mile or so east of the rearmost; I took a careful look all around for enemy fighters, and then turned downward into my dive, arching around back towards them, tensing myself for the bath of anti-aircraft fire as one does when going under an icy shower. I was planning to attack lengthwise, down the line of them, and I leveled out perhaps a hundred feet above the water and about a mile behind them; I took a last glance all around for Navy Zeros, then concentrated on aiming. I was coming fast after my dive, the trees on my left streaking past in a blur.

I held my aim on the first boat as I neared it, waiting for it to grow large enough in my sights. Almost close enough now— aim a little high at first to allow for bullet drop— now!

There's nothing to it, really— you just press in with your thumb. There was the abrupt shattering roar from the guns in my wings and then the eight ghostly white tracers snaking out ahead eagerly, toward the boat and its helpless passengers. They would know nothing more.

Wanting to make the most of my ammunition I broke off after a short burst, not even waiting to see the first bullets strike, then turned and fired at another boat. Not so good; I was turning when I fired and the first bullets threw up their shower of spray to one side of it. I stopped turning and held the nose up in a sideslip to get the sights centered better, and the shower moved over to encompass the boat just as I broke off.

I snapped short bursts into two or three others at close range, just a second or so into each. They were looming in front of me faster than I could possibly shoot at them all. This was terrific!

I had got down too low now, so I nosed up and passed over a few to take good aim at one boatload farther on. I could see the Japs looking at me as I fired— twenty or thirty of them, riding backwards— and then my tracers smacking right into the middle of the close-packed bunch of faces, and for some reason I just held the sights on them, still firing, right up to point-blank.

I zoomed a little then, turning to aim at another boat, and then-WHAM!

It's hard to recall all of what followed, and in what succession. I was conscious of having been hit, harder than I had ever been hit in my life— a quick, cruel blow in the calf of my left leg; I had a momentary glimpse through a big rent in my trousers of two holes in the side of my leg, one small and round, the other a gaping sort of thing an inch wide by a couple of inches long, with raw red and blue flesh and muscle laid open, before the blood welled up and started streaming out.

I was banking hard to the left to flee out over the jungle, more by instinct than plan probably, I was so stunned. Then my mind seemed to start working, and the first thing it told me was that I was in one of the worst jams of my life, for I was nearly a hundred miles from the airdrome, and a weakness of mine is that I tend to faint when I'm hurt and bleeding— and I had never been hurt like this before, and had never bled like this before!

Seemingly with the very thought I started feeling light and sick, the shock and heavy pain overwhelming. I'd grabbed my torn trouser leg above the wound with my left hand, remembering what I'd heard about tourniquets, and twisted on it frantically, trying to stop the blood. Now I glanced down to see if it had done any good, but the blood was still running fast, down my trouser leg, sock, and shoe, and dribbling off to form a sickening bright red puddle in the heel rest— a sort of flat metal trough below the rudder pedal.

This was awful. At this low altitude it would be all over if I fainted for even a few seconds, and now the sight of the blood had made me worse. I looked straight ahead trying to keep my mind off it, but there were blood and bits of flesh spattered over my instrument panel and windshield. My ears were beginning to ring and bright specks floated around the cockpit. I was trying with dreadful urgency to clench my teeth and fight against it without having any strength to do so, saying to myself, "I mustn't faint, I mustn't faint!" Then it was worse and I was having trouble to see, and I thought, panic-stricken, "I am fainting— I mustn't faint— I am fainting!"...

Somehow it passed, after just a few seconds I suppose. I'd had sense enough to lean back, relaxing what I could and drawing deep breaths. The noise of the engine, which had faded nearly away, was back, and the jungle still streaked past just beneath my wings. I still felt terrible, as if I couldn't hold out much longer, wondering wildly if I should shut off my engine and crash-land first. Then I thought of my oxygen supply and let go of the stick long enough to twist the regulator valve on my instrument panel, opening it until I was getting enough oxygen to fly at forty thousand feet. That should help.

I thought I must keep my mind off the wound, so I took time for a careful look around for enemy fighters, saw none, and then noticed that I still had my throttle at cruising setting. I let go of the stick again to reach over and shove it wide open— not daring to let go of my trouser leg with the other hand. If I could just get that bleeding stopped ...

I looked down again to check, and the blood was still running. Not good enough, I realized. I must do something better, and quick. I'm sure I could never do it now, but I was desperate then and it seemed easy. I let go the hold I had on my trouser leg above the wound, grabbed up the torn cloth right over it, twisted it, and then jammed my gloved fist, knuckles first, as deep as I could into the large hole, and held it that way.

The effort, together with the sight of the blood and the thought of what I was doing, brought on my next fainting spell and for a long moment all I could do was sit back, taking deep breaths, controlling the airplane laxly, panic-stricken, trying to keep the awful sickness down and my eyes clear. If I never have another five minutes like those it will be quite soon enough for me!

Somehow that spell passed and things cleared up again. It gave me new confidence that I could make it, and for the first time I thought to check whether my machine was damaged. I glanced at the radiator temperature and oil pressure gauges. They were normal. Thank heavens! The radiator and engine hadn't been hit. Then I checked the fuel gauges. The main tanks were down a reasonable amount for the time I'd been flying, and my reserve was full. It was all comforting, for it meant that nothing important could have been hit except me. I kept looking around for enemy fighters, and scrooching as close down over the trees as I could to keep from being seen.

I don't think I had any more fainting spells, but, as I remember, the next minutes were just long and painful. At last the thick jungle beneath me began to give way to less wooded country, nearly all under water, divided up into rice fields by earthen embankments, with houses here and there and an occasional roadway raised above the level of the water. I realized I must be nearing Palembang, for the only rice-farming land I had noticed was an area south and south-east of there. Then I saw a pall of smoke marking the city itself, a few miles ahead and on my right.

I'd been keeping my mind religiously away from thoughts of my wound since the last fainting spell, for fear that thoughts of it or the sight of it would bring on another, but now I took a chance and looked down, to find, almost incredulously, that the bleeding seemed to have stopped. The red rivulets down my leg and shoe seemed to be stationary, and the puddle of blood in the heel rest was no longer bright red but dark, which meant that there couldn't be any fresh blood on it. The pain, which never had been agonizing, had settled to a heavy ache as from a badly bruised muscle. My hopes of making it really soared.

I passed about five miles south of Palembang, but couldn't see the city itself for the smoke and fires around and in it. Halfway there, I estimated. Now if I just didn't miss the railway and get lost…

My engine was bellowing away, wide open still, and I reached over and throttled it down a little. No use burning it up if I could help it. I kept talking to myself, trying to keep my mind off the wound, and kept looking around and above for signs of enemy planes as well as watching ahead for the railroad, which I should be crossing soon. The weather was worse here and I had to keep altering course to avoid passing through rainstorms, in which I might not notice the railroad when I passed over.

At last there it was, and my anxiety on that score was over. I swung left joyfully and scooted along over the tree-tops beside the tracks, feeling more confident than ever of success. I talked out loud, telling myself, "Only ten minutes more now, old boy, and you're all O.K. You'll sleep in bed tonight, too, and have breakfast in bed tomorrow morning!" That sort of chatter and lots of other silly things, anything to keep my mind away from the wound and how I felt. I thought of friends I'd write to in the hospital and what I'd tell them, and of all kinds of things like that, while the trees streaked by beneath my wings and the long curving miles of railway track unwound out of the distance ahead and spun past and reeled away behind, until all at once the jungle was broken ahead and there was the airdrome!

Getting down was somewhat of a problem, because there are lots of gadgets to work in landing a Hurricane, and I didn't dare to take my left hand out of the wound, for fear my glove should be stuck in it and cause a spasm of pain and bleeding. I decided to try to make it with one hand, cursing the unconventional type of control stick we have on R.A.F. fighters, which you can't handle with your knees like ordinary control sticks.

I flew low over the watch office on the edge of the field, slowly, rocking my wings as a warning that I was in trouble; then pulled up to two or three hundred feet and released the stick long enough to jerk the hydraulic control into wheels down position. A moment later there were a couple of thumps as the wheels locked in their lowered positions, and the two green lights came on in my instrument panel to show me they were down properly. I circled wide to make my approach on the runway, and when I was almost over the field I let go of the stick again to pull the throttle back and shove the hydraulic control into flaps down position, fishtailed a little to get rid of the extra speed I had, and she settled down in a nice glide.

Then I had a little trouble because I hadn't pulled the throttle quite all the way back, so the engine was still idling too fast to allow me to land; I didn't notice it until I was too close to the ground to let go of the stick again and change it. However, I managed to get my left elbow hooked on the throttle while I was leveling off, and pulled it back that way. Then of course I had to go and mess up my landing, bouncing badly. Not being able to use my engine to help recover I had to just keep bouncing, for about one-third of the way across the field, until I didn't have enough speed to bounce any more.

I didn't mind though. The feeling of triumph at having made it safely made the bad landing seem inconsequential! I felt almost boisterous as I taxied up to the watch office.

Netherlands Indies Armed Services Communique:

Batavia, February 16. Early Sunday morning a large-scale bombardment was begun on the Japanese fleet in Banka Strait. American, British, and Netherland aircraft took part in these bombardments.

In the Musi Estuary the Japanese transferred their troops into all kinds of small craft, sloops, motorboats, rowing boats and other local material. The invaders then sailed into various rivers and creeks, continuously harried by our very low-flying fighters and bombers, which played murderous havoc among the thousands of invaders.

Our losses in aircraft and men are not yet known, but it can be taken that they are considerably lower than the extent of the large action would make us expect.

Chapter XIII

"We'll be Back"

There isn't much left to tell. Some of the boys lifted me out of my machine, and Flight Lieutenant S—, a good chap who was doing duty pilot there, put a field dressing on my leg. Then I was packed off in an ambulance to the dressing station, and I had a sinking feeling for a time as I realized they intended to put me in a hospital here, which meant that I'd be in grave danger of being captured by the rapidly advancing enemy.

My worries were short-lived, however, for a telephone call came to the dressing station shortly after I was brought in, saying I was to be sent back out to the drome, at once. I could think of only one reason for that, and I was right. When I arrived back at the drome I found that a Lockheed bomber bound for Java was held up waiting for me at Squadron Leader T—'s intercession.

Two hours later I was safely in bed, three hundred miles from the fighting zone, in the Dutch Military Hospital of Bandoeng, a beautiful city in the mountains of west central Java. I had all that I'd promised myself— a bed to sleep in, with clean sheets, and the prospect of breakfast in bed in the morning! In addition I had a very pretty nurse to look after me.

The nurses were swell, as was the Dutch Army doctor who carefully examined my wound and then said, to my relief, "You are very lucky!"

I had been hit by a half-inch machine-gun bullet, he said — light anti-aircraft fire. And only that morning I had said I didn't think the Japanese anti-aircraft fire was very effective! The bullet must have struck some part of the airplane first, so that it was tumbling over and over when it hit me, with the result that it came out sideways, making the large hole that I had to plug with my fist. It hadn't touched the bone, however, so only flesh and muscle were damaged. The wound gave me surprisingly little pain, and I got along fine. I could hobble around a little at the end of four days.

The morning after I arrived there I overheard one of the nurses, in the hall outside my room, exclaim something in Dutch that sounded like "Singapore iss oberhagen!" Anyway it was close enough so I knew what it meant, and later I learned that the surrender had taken place the day before.

Even though I had known when I left that only a miracle could ever save Singapore, the final news was overwhelming to me. Now the war would last much longer, and many, many more lives would have to be sacrificed to win it. The thought of thousands of those filthy little rats of humans swarming over the beautiful island and city was almost too much. One of them no doubt would be driving my Ford car now— too bad I hadn't set fire to it.

I thought too of the exotic dark-haired girl we'd watched on the lawn of the Sea View that last morning, and wondered what became of her and all the other civilians who were still there when I left.

The first two or three days I spent here at Bandoeng were marvelously peaceful, but things were happening fast and the change was rapid.

With the fall of Singapore and Palembang (which was taken by the enemy the day after I was wounded), the Japs began putting the pressure on Java, and within a few days they made their first air raid on Bandoeng. Some bombers attacked the airdrome on the outskirts of town while a bunch of Navy Zeros fought a dogfight with Brewster Buffaloes of the Dutch Air Force within view of us a few miles away.

After that the raids were virtually a daily affair, and we knew that the invasion of Java would be only a matter of time. We British patients hoped we hadn't escaped from the enemy in Sumatra only to be trapped by them here.

That was how it stood when one morning Doc H—, an R.A.F. flight lieutenant, came into our ward to tell us to hurry and get packed, as we were moving at once. He had fixed up our passage on a hospital ship, for which we will be forever grateful to him.

Get packed! I had nothing to pack, as was true of most of the dozen or so others, for we had lost everything we had. I just put on my shirt and trousers and was ready.

I felt miserable as I went around shaking hands and saying good-bye to my friends among the doctors, nurses, and Dutch patients. They knew as well as I what they were being left to. It was betrayed in the harried looks on their faces, as I hope it was betrayed in shame on mine, but no one spoke of it. They only smiled, bravely if wistfully, and wished me luck. I left my wings with Ann, the little nurse who first took care of me.

That afternoon we departed in a convoy of three ambulances on our trip of a hundred and twenty miles along winding, dusty, hilly country roads that passed through jungles, rubber plantations, irrigated rice farms, and native villages of woven palmetto huts with thatched roofs, all the way from the mountainous country where Bandoeng is located down to Batavia on the seacoast, where we boarded our ship late that evening.

There I met Mickey, whose story of his experiences at Palembang I related in Chapter XI. He had his neck still bandaged and could only talk in a whisper because of the piece of shrapnel in his throat, and was in a very nervous state.

Later we were to pick up a couple of pilots of 175 Squadron, including Stewie, whose story I told in Chapter IX. Our send-off from Batavia next morning was a thirty-minute air raid on the city and harbor. Dive-bombers plastered the docks and vicinity and Navy Zeros roared across low down, machine-gunning ships and patrol boats, chased by pom-pom shells that looked like little red sparks chasing each other across the bay.

At the same time a formation of large bombers made methodical attacks from high level on a cruiser anchored near us, missing it each time and sending up gigantic towers of water that subsided to leave great curtains of muddied mist. We patients who could get around were rushing from one side of the ship to the other, watching the various acts of the show, occasionally throwing ourselves flat when bombs or low-flying airplanes came near. The dive-bombers hit an oil storage tank close to the harbor and set it on fire, too.

The roar of engines, the mad chorus of anti-aircraft guns, the scream of falling bombs, and the crash of the explosions, all combined in a terrific din, while the black smoke and red flames from the blazing oil tank on shore completed the picture and made this the fifth time that I had evacuated a place to the noise of gunfire and bombs, and the sight of the flames and smoke of war.

We sailed about an hour later, and all afternoon the northwest coast of Java was an irregular green panorama bounding the warm blue sea on our left, as our little hospital ship sailed westward from Batavia; the pleasing sight of it, together with the feel of the soft tropical sea breeze, was soothing to the discouraged hearts and aching wounds of us patients as we lay on our mattresses on deck. About dusk we reached the western end of Java and swung southward, into the narrow Soenda Straits which separate it from Sumatra.

After supper I made my way up to the top deck, for a last look at these two countries.

It was nearly dark, and the ship's lights were on — the first time I had ever traveled on a lighted ship. Spotlights illuminated the red crosses on its deck, sides, and funnel.

I sat down on a hatch cover to ease my leg.

The sky was clear and most of the stars were already out. There are medium-sized mountains near this part of the coasts of both Java and Sumatra, and I could see both from where I sat— those of dark Sumatra on our right, already conquered and occupied by the enemy, and those of beautiful Java on our left, doomed to a similar fate in a few more days. They were great dark silhouettes against the stars, silent, and looked, I thought, sad and brooding.

I felt sad, too, and spiritually very tired.

There's no need denying that I was terribly disillusioned by much of what I had seen and experienced out here — things that I have avoided or passed over in this story because it isn't in my province as a member of the forces to speak of them, and because I could only do harm by telling about them now. The enemy don't advertise their failings either, you know.

Doubtless you have seen references to this in the press, so there's no harm in admitting that I saw many things out here that were very bad. The humiliating memories of them, and the overwhelming realization of the great defeat we had suffered with the consequent imperiling of our entire cause, after all the bright hopes I'd had when I came out here less than a month before, combined to make me more discouraged and heartsick than I had ever been before.

Besides, my leg was aching again.

Of the forty-eight beautiful new Hurricanes we had flown to Singapore, scarcely a dozen were left the day I was wounded. No doubt they were all gone now. From Mickey I gathered that little more than half the pilots were alive, and we had little to show. We had stopped our enemies nowhere.

I reflected that in two and a half months these new enemies had overrun Malaya, Singapore, and Sumatra in rapid succession. They were winning in the Philippines and other places, and I thought to myself, "Where are we going to stop them?"

And then another thought came that made me shiver. "Are we going to stop them?"

Was it possible that we were really losing this war? Were these perhaps the last days of our civilization?

Surely I had seen out here most of the things that had preceded the fall of other great civilizations — the softness and decadence that come from easy living — the lack of appreciation for the good things of life that comes from the too easy attainment of them — the failure to appreciate freedom that comes from taking it for granted too long.

It was only a mood, a discouraged, dismayed sort of mood, that came from the too recent, too vivid memories of all these "things that were bad," which tended to push older memories of bigger and better and much more important things out of my perspective and give me a distorted view, as an ant in a burning bush might think the world was on fire.

I began to realize this, as I sat there letting the cool night breeze and the soothing endless throb of the engines comfort and reassure me, and gradually my view of it all seemed to broaden.

After all, though we were beaten in this theater of the war, it was only an outpost of the British Empire, garrisoned by a fraction of Britain's strength, which had been overwhelmed by almost the full strength of another great nation while Britain herself was engaged in a death struggle with Germany and Italy, almost half-way around the world from here.

I, if anyone, should certainly know that the "things that were bad" out here were not typically British, for I had served more than a year in England, where the universal fighting spirit and loyalty had made me feel very inferior. The people there were anything but decadent, and the miserable creatures who had let down their King and country so woefully out here were no more true British than the fifth columnists and saboteurs in my own country were true Americans.

I thought of the tremendous fighting forces being built up in England, readying themselves for the time when they could strike and let all the Axis know what the real British people will do when aroused.

And I remembered, too, the quotation the Prime Minister used in one of his speeches: "Westward look— the land is bright!"

Yes, it was tragic that America had entered the war, but now that my people were in it they would brook nothing. We Americans aren't decadent either, although with a few more years of coddling we might have been.

I began seeing things in a better light, a light which seemed to show the Rising Sun very near its zenith.

Darkness had set about our ship now, but in a few hours it would begin to get light again. Another kind of darkness was settling over all the Far East, but in a few months, or a few years…?

I stood up and started for the stairway, and at the top took a last long look at each of the two coastlines, very dark now against the sky.

I thought to myself, "We'll be back."

Publisher's Note

The letters which follow, written by the author after the period covered by the foregoing narrative, are published in order to complete this account of the fighting career of the first American pilot in combat with the R.A.F.

Letters Home

Hospital Ship #...
At Sea, March 1, 1942

Dear Folks:

There's very little I can think of to write about, but I've lots and lots of time so will probably be able to think of enough to fill out a letter.

My leg has been healing incredibly fast, and now, two weeks from the day I was wounded, I can walk perfectly normally. Just have to be careful about putting a side strain on my foot or leg, as that causes it to hurt a little. Actually, the wound looks the same as ever. I suppose it's building out from the inside. It's perfectly clean though, and they only dress it every third day now.

Just in case this letter gets to you before any other word. I'll explain that I was wounded by a bullet through part of the calf of my leg, about eight inches below the knee, from Japanese anti-aircraft fire. It was only a flesh and muscle wound, the bullet missing all important parts of my leg. I never had any shock or fever, nor bad pain. While I have good use of my leg already, I imagine it will be some time before the wound is actually filled and healed up.

Anyway, they decided I wouldn't be much use fighting Japs for a while, so after a few days in hospital, they packed me off on this boat, and I'm not sure yet just where I'll end up.

One thing interesting about this trip is that we sail with lights full on at night, and no attempt at concealment. Our protection is the red cross on the funnel of the ship, lit up by floodlights. There is also a big red cross over the deck and red crosses on the sides. Otherwise the ship is painted white except for a green stripe around the middle of it. These are the recognized international markings and so far the Japs have respected hospital ships, which puts even them on a little better level than the Nazis.

Now I'm getting nearly to the end of these two sheets of Red Cross issue paper that I asked for, and there just isn't anything more I can think of to talk about, so guess I might as well close.

Will write some more as soon as we get somewhere and have something to talk about.

Much love to all,
Art.

Trichinopoly, Madras Pres. (India)
April 16, 1942

Dear Mother, Dad, and All:

I brought this stationery along when I left Delhi Sunday, planning to write at the first opportunity, and here it's Thursday already! I've been traveling most of the time since, except for the day I took off to visit the Taj Mahal, and still have another day of it but have to wait until morning for a train connection.

By the time I've finished this trip I think I shall have had enough of Indian railway travel to do me for quite a while. The only way to do it is to have one outfit of clothes to wear while you're on the train and keep the rest tightly locked up, and resign yourself to living like a bum until you reach your destination. There's no use attempting to keep clean or to keep dust out of your eyes, ears, nose, and throat as well as your food and all your clothes. It's insufferably hot through most of the daylight hours, so that you and your clothes are damp and consequently dust sticks to you and forms a coating of mud all over. I've been provided "first class" tickets all the way, which means that I have a "sleeping compartment." This amounts to sharing a compartment the width of the car and about ten feet long with three other passengers, there being sort of an upholstered bench for each to sit or lie on (two upper and two lower). The trains are rough, noisy, and slow.

Nevertheless the trip has been more interesting than I can tell, for it's given me a chance to see what a lot of the country looks like and what some of the people are like. It certainly is an education. I've taken something like fifteen rolls of snapshots — one hundred twenty pictures — so far on the trip, having resolved to build up a good picture record of it.

Outside of the fact that I'm in perfect health, I guess there isn't anything in the line of news. There's nothing left of my wound but a couple scars now, and I've had perfect use of my leg for some time.

Will write more soon. Much love to all.

Art

Royal Air Force Station
Ceylon, April 21, 1942

Dear Mother, Dad, and All:

Well here I'm back on the job again at last, and it does feel good to be making myself useful again after lying around for so long. I had a tumultuous welcome when I walked in on the boys here. They didn't know that I was coming at all. Most of them I hadn't seen since the day I was wounded, and we had lots of jabber fests exchanging our stories. Some of the boys had amazing adventures in escaping.

Wednesday, April 22

Can't remember just what happened to interrupt me at this point yesterday, but will try to keep going this time. I received a cable from Bob last evening, beginning with the words "Congratulations DFC" which is the first definite intimation I've had that it has come thru! The boys here said that I had been recommended for it, but I've never had any notification. I can only conjecture that it was gazetted in England and the news got over to you folks via press reports, and the notice is still on its way back here. Needless to say it was quite a thrill! Certainly an incentive. I'm afraid it's going to cost me some money though, as the gang insist that I've got to throw a party for it!

Bob also said that the last letter you'd received was from Sudan. There should be some more stringing along, I hope, as I wrote from Singapore, Sumatra, and Java in February. He also said that my book [TALLY-HO! Yankee in a Spitfire] was in its fifth printing and that a separate English edition is being published, which sounds like it must be fairly successful. I'm still working on my new book, and am shopping to buy a typewriter as I guess the Japs got my other one. Have been writing in long hand and will make the final job on a typewriter.

This is a rather nice country, much nicer than India. It's terribly hot and dusty in most parts of India. Here it's pretty hot, but the climate is damp enough so it isn't dusty, and the whole country is very rich and green and beautiful. About the only agricultural product is rice, and there are "rice paddies" everywhere — little plots of ground a few hundred feet square surrounded by little low dykes to keep the water in when the land is supposed to be flooded. In addition there are lots of tea, rubber, and copra plantations. The natives are for the most part darker skinned than in India, many of them a great deal like negroes except that they are very small. Transportation within town is by either rickshaw or taxi, the rickshaw coolies taking one person each.

Here's hoping this finds all of you well and happy as I am.

Much love to all.

Art

Royal Air Force Station
Ceylon, May 10, 1942

Dear Folks·

Here's another whole week rolled by without my writing, and I had promised myself I was going to write twice a week! I don't know-why I never get down to it. Of course I'm spending a lot of time on my book, and it seems like something turns up for me to do or there is some distraction, every time I get set to write.

My big news of the week is that my D.F.C. finally came through, on Monday. Sunday afternoon an official from Group Headquarters, who was visiting the C.O., told him that it was on the way. So that night, at a little Sunday evening party in the Mess, Denny cut an imitation ribbon out of a piece of pasteboard, drew stripes on it in ink, and pinned it on me! The reason I didn't get it for so long was that it was awarded in London and the notification hadn't found its way through all the channels and mails to get out here.

Anyway next morning I went into town to do some shopping, and the first item on my list of things to get was "ribbon." I had to go to several places before I found it. Every tailor shop had all sorts of Army and Navy medal ribbons, but the Air Force being something new out here, most of them didn't know what D.F.C. was. Finally I found a little tailor shop that had an extra large assortment and the fellow, after leafing through a large stack of envelopes, containing different kinds of ribbons, at last turned one up marked "D.F.C." Sure enough, it contained a little strip of ribbon, and I bought two inches of it, enough for two brooches. They didn't have any brooches so I went to another shop and succeeded in buying one, and the fellow sewed the ribbon on, all for 25 cents (about 8 cents American) so feeling like celebrating I gave him a whole rupee (30 cents American) and told him to keep the change.

Then I went around doing the rest of my shopping, feeling awfully conspicuous and imagining that everyone was looking at my breast where I had the brooch pinned! Then I ran into one of the pilots of my squadron who had just arrived by train, having been away on leave. He of course didn't know about it, and his eyes nearly popped out of his head.

The announcement was in our Squadron Orders for the day, in the official language: "His Majesty the King has been graciously pleased to award the following decoration: No... Squadron... F/O A. G. Donahue: — D.F.C."

I believe I described the D.F.C. in a letter a year or so ago— it's silk ribbon, purple and white. I probably won't receive the medal itself for a long time, as is usually the case.

There doesn't seem to be much else of interest to tell about this time. Yesterday's big news was of what sounds like a very important naval victory over the Japs in the Pacific, with at least two aircraft carriers sunk as well as other warships. We are expecting the onset of the monsoon season in another week, which means almost continuous rain, so that if I stay here I'll probably be more fat and idle than ever. Will close now, hoping you're all well and fit as I am.

Love to all,
Art

Bombay
June 14, 1942

Dear Folks,

Well here I am, back in the "Somewheres east of Suez" land again. Can't see as it's any cleaner or better in any other way than before, either.

I shot another dozen or so rolls of film on the way here, so that now I must have well over two hundred snaps of every kind of people and every phase of life that I've seen, as well as landscapes, temples, etc., by the score.

... I got a copy of "TALLY-HO!" in a book store here a couple days ago. It was the only one they had left. In the largest bookstore in town, they were sold out of it, having had a dozen copies to start with. These all came from America, and they are expecting some of the English edition soon. Am sending the copy I bought up to Poona, to a very close friend of mine in the hospital there.

Suppose all America is jubilant now over the naval victories in the Pacific. Things surely do look brighter just now than they did a couple months ago. Hope they haven't dimmed any by the time you get this.

... Suppose by the time this gets there you boys and girls will be in the middle of your vacation, or past it. Have a good time, anyway.

Love to all,
Art

An R.A.F. Station on the English Channel
Aug. 26, 1942

Dear Folks:

I wrote to St. Charles only a couple days ago, but it was such a short note that I feel obliged to try and write a decent letter now that I have time, and give an account of what I've been doing with myself prior to coming to work.

Well, first of all, after I got back to England (about Monday, the 10th) I had to spend a couple of days around Air Ministry, getting interviewed, etc. Then I was given seven days to do as I liked before reporting again to get my posting. So I spent some time shopping and doing some chasing around in connection with my new book and then took a quick trip down here to check up on my old friends. I stayed over one night here and went back the next day, but it was the result of that visit that I was asked for by the C.O. of the squadron and eventually posted here.

On Friday of that week I had quite a big day. To begin with, I was invited, along with three other R.A.F. boys (Americans), to have coffee with Ben Lyon and Bebe Daniels at their house, where we worked out the script for the radio interview which I hope you heard. That was in the morning and about noon we went over to Broadcasting House and made the recordings. Afterwards we made Bebe autograph our copies of our scripts. She and Ben Lyon are, I suppose, a rather unusual pair in that they are two actors who married and made a go of it, and are still together after the close of their careers in the movies. They seem very attached to each other, live quietly in a very nice house just outside the main part of town, and devote their time to radio work, mainly for the forces. They have two very nice children, whose pictures they showed us, who are staying with relatives in California.

In the afternoon I was invited to a sort of open house tea for Americans at Noel Coward's. There were probably twenty or more Americans — R.A.F., U.S. Army and U.S. Navy men — there, but he managed to circulate among all of us and was about the most accomplished host in that respect that I have seen.

Next day I met Charles Collingwood, the C.B.S. correspondent in London. He'd invited me to have lunch with him, as he wanted to talk about a possible broadcast. I met him in Broadcasting House just before noon and "sat in" on his news broadcast to the U.S. It was very interesting. We were in the studio ahead of time and they carried out tests to make sure the contact was O.K. with New York. They left the transmitters on until actual broadcast time, or several minutes. Transmission is via radio beam directed at New York. He talked back and forth with New York as easily as if they were phoning from the next room. Their replies came to us through a loudspeaker in the studio. We could hear the fellows in the New York office chatting back and forth, walking about, opening and shutting the door, etc. If anything ever tended to make me homesick, that certainly did— to actually hear those things going on in America! (This was while waiting for the actual broadcast.)

He didn't plan a definite broadcast, as he wants to wait for the right opportunity. He apparently wanted most to get acquainted and make sure I was willing to cooperate when the opportunity came. He's had plenty of interesting experiences — was in Holland during the winter of 1939-40, and up to the time of the invasion of Holland.

… My posting later came through for me to come down here, and I've been here ever since. This letter has now dragged out for three days, so I'll try to make a big spurt and finish it today (8/29). Chief cause of all the delay is that I am acting C.O. of the squadron for a couple weeks or so while my C.O. is on other duties. It started out with nothing for me to do except sit in the office and try to look intelligent, but then some troubles came up and for the last couple days I've been busy as the dickens. I think it will ease up again tho. The work is all new and interesting for men — all manner of office and administration problems to take care of — but cramps my style in that I don't get to fly as much.

That seems to be all I can think of to talk about now. Suppose harvest is about over and silo filling in the offing. Wish I could be there to lend a hand, but maybe it won't be too long. Look after yourselves.

Much love to all.

Art

R.A.F. Station in England
September 5, 1942

Dear Folks:

Have just finished lunch and arrived back at the office half an hour ahead of time, so will utilize the time before the staff arrive in getting this letter started. (Am still acting C.O. of my squadron and probably will be for another week or so because the regular C.O. is away on another job.) I've learned quite a bit about R.A.F. administration since I took over the job ten days ago and it's getting to be fun. The only disadvantage is that it's a little hard for me to fly as much as I like to, but then I have the C.O.'s prerogative of being able to select the choicer jobs when I do want to fly and also I have the pick of any airplane I want to use, which is all quite nice.

I haven't had any more letters since the one from Minneapolis dated July 24, but am hoping expectantly. Am glad to know that some of the ones I mailed from far comers of the globe are gradually arriving there. Have you received the one I sent from Ceylon, telling about my trip to the Taj Mahal? Not only do I think you'll find it interesting, but there is a complete collection of all types of Ceylon stamps on the envelope!

I was interested, Blanche and Ora, to learn that you had a chance to see a Spitfire and a Messerschmitt. Very sorry you didn't get to see the Spit flying, as they are such a beautiful airplane in the air. Anyway I presume you now know what I meant when I referred to the high-pitched moan of a Messerschmitt. Strange, I just can't imagine either of those airplanes being in Minnesota. It's a sacrilege.

… Well, I think my plans are definite enough for the next few months so I can risk telling you this much, that the chances are four to one that I'll be with you for Christmas this year! I have the furlough coming and could take it now if I wished to, but prefer to wait until then. I hope to have a month in the States, possibly more, so don't go planning any celebration but keep it in your hope chest anyway. Next week I expect to learn more about what details I can work out, and altogether the prospects are looking most favorable. I don't dare let myself think about it too much, or I start losing interest in my job, and while I've said nothing before you can be sure that I have been playing my cards with that in view for quite a long time. Anyway, here's hoping.

I haven't learned much about the crops there in the letters I've got so far (naturally enough) except that there was a good hay crop and Ora remarked that you had a lot of pigs this year, Dad. That sounds good, altho I haven't much idea what prices are like now.

I have just been around behind one of the buildings and saw an aircraft hand unearthing a good two bushels of lovely new potatoes, good sized, from a little three-cornered plot of soil between the building and a couple sidewalks, not more than twenty feet in each direction! It's really amazing the amount of food that's being grown off these little odds and ends of ground as a result of the government's campaign to get every possible square foot of ground cultivated. Now we pilots are trying to get organized to keep our own chickens here. You see the government has rationed eggs down to about one per week per person, except that operational pilots are permitted an extra one or two if obtainable. However, any person may keep up to two hens and have all the eggs they lay. If you have more than two hens you have to sell the eggs. So we are planning to each have two hens if we can arrange a place to keep them.

Another concession that has now been initiated for operational pilots is that we each have a half pint of whole milk per day (very rich too) in addition to normal rations which are enough for all cereals, tea, coffee, etc. All in all, the food is better than at this time last year. Not as much meat, perhaps, but I never was much of a meat eater anyway; and of course there is no white bread, but the bread normally used is about halfway between white and graham, and very delicious. There is more than plenty to eat by far.

Guess I better close this if I don't want it to be overweight.

Much love to all.

Art

R.A.F. Station in England
September, 1942

Dear Mr. Donahue:

Let me begin by saying how much we miss Art. No-one who knew him could help liking and admiring him and it was a great blow to those of us who had been associated with him since the early days when we learned that he had failed to return from a patrol. All the boys in his squadron wish to join me in expressing our great sympathy to you and all his family.

The censorship does not allow me to go into any details of his last flight, but we do know through radio messages that he badly damaged and probably destroyed an enemy bomber before he himself got into difficulties.

I hope that you will keep in touch with me and perhaps — after we've won this war — we will be able to meet and I'll be able to give you an idea of how much we all thought of Art and his *Message from Minnesota*. I'll let you know of any changes in address.

Yours sincerely,

F/Lt. F. D. M

AIR MINISTRY,
London,
20th July, 1943.

Madam,

I am commanded by the Air Council to state that in view of the lapse of time and the absence of any further news regarding your brother. Flight Lieutenant A. G. Donahue, D.F.C., since the date on which he was reported missing, they must regretfully conclude that he has lost his life, and his death has now been presumed, for official purposes, to have occurred on the 11th September, 1942.

The Council desire me to express again their sympathy with you in the anxiety which you have suffered, and in your bereavement.

I am, Madam,

Your obedient Servant,

J. Smith

Made in the USA
Middletown, DE
29 November 2017